D1232509

40
Devotions
for Women

Fearless and Free

BroadStreet
PUBLISHING

BroadStreet Publishing® Group, LLC
Savage, Minnesota, USA
BroadStreetPublishing.com

Fearless and Free: 40 Devotions for Women

ISBN 978-1-4245-5716-5 (faux leather)
ISBN 978-1-4245-5717-2 (e-book)

Stock or custom editions of BroadStreet Publishing titles may be purchased in bulk for educational, business, ministry, fundraising, or sales promotional use. For information, please email info@broadstreetpublishing.com.

Cover by Chris Garborg at garborgdesign.com
Interior by Katherine Lloyd at theDESKonline.com

Printed in China
18 19 20 21 22 5 4 3 2 1

This book compiles the stories of some women of the faith who have served their Master throughout the centuries, often behind the scenes. The women you will read about in these pages are some of the heroines that impacted my dear wife's life. We give them honor.

It is my great honor to dedicate this book to the legacy and lineage of another great woman of God in this generation who stopped for the one, whose walk matched her talk, and who lived a life devoted to Jesus. It is my deepest honor to dedicate *Fearless and Free* in the memory of Michal Ann Goll, a friend and servant of God.

Her loving husband,
James W. Goll

Contents

Foreword

My late wife, Michal Ann, was an amazing and truly inspiring woman and a deeply devoted lover of Christ all the days of her life. She embodied the definition of what being a true Christian is—one who had a personal relationship with the living Savior and one who loved back to the degree that she was first loved. Michal Ann (Willard) Goll was the most pure and real believer I ever had the pleasure of knowing in this life.

This forty-day devotional journal is a compilation of the best from her three books in the *Women on the Front Lines* series: *A Call to Courage, A Call to the Secret Place,* and *A Call to Compassion.* You will enjoy the depth of compassion found within each daily devotion along with the peace and comfort you will feel as you allow God to immerse you in His love and grace.

Michal Ann wrote about women who were committed to others and to spreading the love of the gospel throughout the world in practical ways. May you be empowered to share His living Word with others as you meditate on the lives of these Christian role models of courage, devotion, and compassion. As Michal Ann always said, "We each must build our own Hall of Heroes of the Faith." In these pages you will be introduced to some of "Annie's" inductees into her Hall of Heroes who inspired her life.

And now, I introduce you to one of mine—Michal Ann Goll—who has joined the great cloud of witnesses.

—James W. Goll

Fearless and Free

> And we know [with great confidence] that God
> [who is deeply concerned about us] causes all things to work
> together [as a plan] for good for those who love God, to those
> who are called according to His plan and purpose.
>
> ROMANS 8:28

I was raised in a devout Methodist family. My grandmother was a sweet, wonderful woman who loved God. Even when she was suffering from cancer she always challenged me and my cousins to put Jesus first in our lives. I cherish that rich heritage from which I received a deep deposit of the Word of God.

However, I did not understand the ways of the Spirit. For a long time after I married Jim (James), I tried to hang onto his coattails; I simply followed what he was doing. Unknowingly, I was comparing my walk with God to Jim's walk, thinking that his was better than mine. God did not see it that way, and He told me so.

One day the Lord said to me, "Ann, you can't hold onto Jim's coattails; hold onto Mine. I am your God! I created you, and I am jealous over you. I won't settle for a relationship through your husband; I want a relationship with you."

He desires the same for each of us. We cannot relate to Him through anyone else—spouse, pastor, parents, friends, or anyone else.

Our God is a personal God!

We are His beloved and we are beautiful in His eyes. He sees us through the precious blood of Jesus, His Son. He doesn't see our faults; rather, He sees only Jesus' righteousness covering us. Instead of sin, He sees the beauty of a forgiven soul. We are beautiful to Him when we're sweating, or when we're lying on the floor in deep travail, or when we're crying with runny noses because God is touching a hurting heart. We are beautiful to Him whether we're shaking, trembling, or jumping. We are beautiful to Him when we are at home with our hearts breaking and we think no one knows or cares.

God looks for the beauty of the heart. I believe that any time we bring life into the world or into some needy soul is a time of unparalleled beauty in God's eyes. God loves life! Consider for a moment the appearance and condition of a woman in childbirth: vulnerable, painful, difficult. Most of us who have been through it don't want to be reminded of our appearance! God, however, tells us to look at the heart of the issue.

Our approval from God doesn't depend on whether or not our fingernails are polished, our hair is combed, or our houses are neat and tidy with everything in order. God looks at the heart. He created each of us as unique individuals with a fragrance all our own, and He waits in longing to smell that fragrance rising to Him. He loves us and fashioned us to be creative according to how He has gifted us. Let God release you to be who He made you to be—a creative individual free from intimidation and the fear of others.

Have you ever found yourself at a buffet and, as you pick up your plate to go through the line, you check to see how much food everyone else is taking, then take the same amount? You don't want to take "too much." After all, you have to be careful how you present yourself, right? That's intimidation speaking!

I've got good news for you—God has a buffet all laid out, and He wants you to take the biggest plate you can find and load it up. There are all kinds of breads, pastries, salads and vegetables, luscious fruits, and scrumptious desserts. Wow, what a feast! He wants you to pull your chair right up to the table and dig in because the table is spread for *you.*

Reflect & Pray

1. Fear paralyzes the brain and causes negativity. How does the opposite of fear positively contribute to a healthy state of mind?

2. What was your greatest fear as a child? Have you completely overcome that fear? Why or why not?

3. What is your current greatest fear? Take a moment to pray, giving that fear to God for disposal.

4. Consider that "greater is He who is in you than he who is in the world" (1 John 4:4 NASB). How does this affect fears you may have and how you handle them?

Dear God, I know you don't want me to be afraid of my situations or circumstances. Please give me the confidence to overcome life's challenges, for I realize that people who possess such knowledge possess power. In Jesus' name, amen.

Dare to Dream

"For I know the plans and thoughts that I have for you,"
says the LORD, "plans for peace and well-being and
not for disaster, to give you a future and a hope."

JEREMIAH 29:11

*W*e've got to be free to see, but we can't see if we're bound up in fear. Have you ever been introduced to someone and not caught his or her name because you were so concerned about what you were going to say in response? That's intimidation. Once you are free of it, you can look at someone and think about that person rather than worrying about yourself. In that way, you can be God's hands and God's voice to people and build bridges of love, not fear.

Getting rid of fear and intimidation means getting out of yourself and into Christ, moving from concern over how you look or what you are going to say to asking, "Lord, what do you have for this person?" It is when you get out of yourself that you become truly free. Learning to be free is a lifelong process, but in Christ you have everything you need and it is never too late to begin.

Years ago, I was scheduled to speak at a women's conference in Kansas City on the theme "Overcoming Intimidation." At that time, I had not spoken at many conferences and still felt insecure. I knew that I had to conquer the enemy of intimidation that was coming against me if I were to succeed at this conference. I felt like I needed a lot of prayer time in order to prepare, but the only "quiet" times I had came in fifteen-minute segments while I drove back and forth between home and the school. On the Friday that the conference began, just a few hours before the first meeting, my final, desperate prayer was, "God, let me do this with no fear!"

As soon as I uttered the words I saw a picture in my mind of me wearing a T-shirt with the words *No Fear* across the front. I said to God, "All right, as I speak on Saturday morning I will envision *No Fear* written across my heart, guarding me. In faith, I will believe that you will accomplish this!"

When I told Jim about it later that evening, he insisted that I had to get a "No Fear" T-shirt and wear it. I had no time for shopping though, so he went while I was at the Friday night meeting. I returned home to find laid out on the kitchen counter two T-shirts and two hats with "No Fear" on the front. One set was for me, the other for Jim. Inside the rim of my hat, this sentence was written: "Don't let your fears stand in the way of your dreams."

After years of trying to deal with my fears and after many, many dreams through which God had given me hope, the time had come for me to apply what I had been learning. God was saying, "Gird your mind with the dreams I have placed in you and go, girl!"

I want to issue this challenge to you: Dare to dream! Open your heart in a fresh way and ask God to put a dream there. Ask Him to dust off the promise book with your name on it and make those promises real and fresh to you!

Don't let your fears stand in the way of your dreams! Take out the spike of intimidation and, like the Israelite woman Jael did to the Philistine Sisera in Judges 4, drive it into the enemy's head and kill the plans and schemes he has devised against you. We must be ruthless with the devil; he surely has no mercy on us!

Reflect & Pray

1. What are two dreams you have? What fears may be keeping you from these dreams or from dreaming with God about your future?

2. If you write *No Fear* across your heart today, how will your tomorrows be different?

3. Write Jeremiah 29:11 in your own words, concentrating on the fact that God knows the plans He has for you.

4. What is the difference between fear and worry? What does God say about them? (See Matthew 6:25–34.)

"Yes, though I walk through the [deep, sunless] valley of the shadow of death, I will fear or dread no evil, for You are with me; Your rod [to protect] and Your staff [to guide], they comfort me" (Psalm 23:4). Dear Lord, thank you for your daily protection and guidance. I will praise your name forever. In Jesus' name, amen.

Day 3

Annie Get Your Gun

> For our struggle is not against flesh and blood
> [contending only with physical opponents], but against
> the rulers, against the powers, against the world forces
> of this [present] darkness, against the spiritual forces
> of wickedness in the heavenly (supernatural) places.
>
> EPHESIANS 6:12

Years ago God spoke to me in a dream about the importance of being thoroughly prepared to do battle with the enemy. The images were so vivid and intense that they have remained with me ever since. In my dream I was inside the comfortable old farmhouse of my childhood. Normally full of warmth, charm, family love, and belonging, the house was now a place of fear and panic.

I was alone in an upstairs bedroom and an intruder had entered the house. Spread out on the bed before me were several handguns of different styles and calibers, along with bullets for each. The intruder began coming up the stairs. My mind screamed, *Which one? Which one?* I fumbled with the weapons, trying frantically to figure out which bullets went with which gun so that I could load one of them and use it to defend myself. Before I could do so, the bedroom door burst open and the intruder entered pointing a gun at me. Rushing over to the bed, he quickly overpowered me and dragged me to the floor. Then he was on top of me, and I was fighting desperately to get him off.

My dream ended at that point, leaving me with a terrible ache in my heart. I realized that I did not know the weapons of my warfare. Oh, I knew that I had some, but I wasn't familiar enough with them to use them effectively. I didn't even know which bullet went with which gun, much less have any of the guns loaded and ready. How could I possibly be prepared for attacks from the enemy? I couldn't very well say to him, "Wait a minute! You can't come after me yet. I have to load my gun!"

This started me on a major quest of asking the Lord, "Please, God, show me what my spiritual weapons are and how to use them. Help me to be ready to use them against the enemy whenever he comes against me." I needed to be a trick shooter like Annie Oakley, as skilled with my weapons as she was with hers!

Courage on the front lines of faith requires a thorough knowledge of the spiritual weapons and other resources that we have, as well as supreme devotion to and confidence in the One for whom we fight and who fights for us, taking our battles upon Himself.

We can be encouraged in the assurance that God's banner is over us, His blessings are upon us, and His boldness is in us.

Reflect & Pray

1. What spiritual weapons has God given to you? Which do you use when the enemy tries to overpower you? Which do you want to use more?

2. Read 1 Thessalonians 5:8 and write what this armor of God means to you in your battle against evil.

3. All of us go through bad experiences, and if we are not careful, Satan uses them to eat away at our faith. What can you do to keep Satan from poisoning your thoughts?

4. Meditate on this verse: "The LORD is merciful and gracious, Slow to anger and abounding in compassion and loving-kindness. He will not always strive with us, Nor will He keep His anger forever" (Psalm 103:8–9).

Dear Lord and Savior, thank you for your strength and power. Teach me how to keep my spiritual weapons loaded and ready. I will remember that you said, "Little children (believers, dear ones), you are of God and you belong to Him and have [already] overcome them [the agents of the antichrist]; because He who is in you is greater than he (Satan) who is in the world [of sinful mankind]" (1 John 4:4). In Jesus' name, amen.

Day 4

Courage for the Cause:
Joan of Arc (1412-1431)

> "Things which the eye has not seen and the ear has not heard,
> And which have not entered the heart of man, All that God
> has prepared for those who love Him [who hold Him in
> affectionate reverence, who obey Him, and who gratefully
> recognize the benefits that He has bestowed]."

1 CORINTHIANS 2:9

It was in the midst of political unrest and social upheaval that Joan appeared. Born in 1412 in northeastern France, Joan was the youngest in a family of five. Although skilled in sewing and spinning, she never learned to read or write. From a very early age she displayed an unusually deep devotion to God. She spent hours absorbed in prayer and was known to have a tender heart for the poor and needy.

From her childhood on, Joan simply loved God. She never received any theological training and knew very little about the formal structures and official doctrines of the Roman Catholic Church—the only church in France at that time. All Joan knew was that when she went to mass, God met her there. God can come into any church, any building, any worship setting—formal or informal—to meet with people who love Him and are hungry for His presence.

When she was thirteen, Joan experienced her first heavenly visitation: a blaze of bright light accompanied by a voice. She received numerous such visitations during the months that followed and gradually discerned the identities of those who spoke to her. Joan identified one of them as Michael the archangel; St. Catherine of

Alexandria and St. Margaret of Antioch, both early Christian martyrs, were the others.

Although these may seem to be strange messengers to modern minds, remember that in the case of Michael, angelic visitations have biblical precedent. At first Joan's "voices" told her such things as to be a good girl and obey her parents. However, over the course of three years the messages began to change. She had dreams of horses running in battle and of herself being led away with an army of men. During this time she gradually became aware of the call of God on her life. He seemed to be telling her that she was to go to the aid of the disinherited Charles, the true king of France; drive the English away from Orleans and out of the country, and lead the procession to see Charles enthroned. At first she resisted: "I'm just a girl. I have no education and no training in military skills. Who's going to listen to me?" Her voices continued, however, and became more and more insistent.

Under the insistent direction of her "voices," Joan presented herself and her mission to the commander of Charles' forces in the neighboring town. The commander showed contempt for Joan and her ideas, telling the cousin who had accompanied her to, "Take her home to her father and give her a good whipping."[1]

Joan's visitations continued, her "voices" becoming increasingly urgent. Joan traveled in men's clothing, probably for modesty and practicality. Charles, not knowing what to make of this teenage girl who was coming to see him, decided to test Joan by disguising himself and surrounding himself with attendants. However, when Joan was brought in, she somehow immediately recognized him and addressed him as the king.

Joan had such an incredible presence of the Lord on her that she drew people to her everywhere she turned. By the time she arrived on the field, Charles' army was at a very low point; they were exhausted, defeated, discouraged, and disillusioned. Many of the soldiers had begun to desert. Then Joan appeared, proclaiming that she had a vision from God to raise an army for their nation and for Him. As Joan's presence became known, soldiers began to rush to her side by the thousands.

As miraculous as it seems, the soldiers agreed as one body to come into holy living and purity. Joan had absolutely no training in military operations or strategy, but God gave her battle plans on the field. Some of the generals were still not completely convinced, however, and tried to trick her by following other strategies. God revealed to Joan what was going on, and she challenged the generals: "In God's Name, the advice of Our Lord is wiser and more certain than yours. You thought to deceive me, but it is you who are deceived, for I bring you the best help that ever came to any soldier or to any city."[2]

Within a week they had captured all the English forts surrounding the city. In July 1429, Charles VII was solemnly crowned king with Joan standing by as a witness. Although the principal purpose of her mission had been accomplished, Joan remained with the army throughout the rest of the summer. Her "voices" continued to speak to her, telling her that she would be taken prisoner. In May 1430, the commander of the city accidentally raised the drawbridge while Joan and many of her soldiers were still outside. She was pulled from her horse and made a prisoner of war. Charles VII and his advisors did nothing to try to rescue her. The English, on the other hand, were desperate to get their hands on her.

The English condemned Joan to death as a witch and a heretic. To this end they claimed that Joan's "voices" were satanic in nature and that the only way she could have defeated them in battle was with the help of the powers of darkness. Joan's practice of wearing male dress was also used against her as evidence of her heresy.

Imagine how you would feel in Joan's place: a young woman not yet out of your teens, unable to read or write and without any formal religious training of any kind, being examined and questioned about fine points of religion, faith, theology, and the church by men determined to find something with which to condemn you. Yet Joan stood firm because God held her up. He was her defense and her strong tower, and He gave her the wisdom and the words to answer every question. The record of her trial leaves little room to doubt either her absolute devotion to God or the courage with which she stood for Him.

Joan was turned over for execution by burning at the stake. The execution was carried out on May 30, 1431. As the flames rose around her Joan called out for the cross. When it was held up before her, she called repeatedly on the name of Jesus, forgiving those who had wronged her and pouring out words of love and devotion to Him.[3]

Reflect & Pray

1. When was the last time you demonstrated courage? Write about that time and how it made you feel.
2. What convictions and passion do you have that would cause you to stand against all odds?
3. What do you think about the voices that Joan of Arc heard? Do you believe people hear God's voice today? Why or why not?
4. Is there a cause for which you would consider giving up your career, wealth, even your life? Write your reasons for doing so.

Dear Lord, when considering Joan of Arc, her courage is almost unbelievable. I know you empower men and women to do incredible things in your name. Please empower me for your name's sake. In Jesus' name, amen.

Faithful unto Death:
Vibia Perpetua (AD 182–203)

"Blessed [comforted by inner peace and God's love] are those
who are persecuted for doing that which is morally right, for
theirs is the kingdom of heaven [both now and forever]."

MATTHEW 5:10

Vibia Perpetua, twenty-two years old, came from a good family,
yet she was imprisoned for refusing to make sacrifices for the
prosperity of the Roman emperor. It is possible that Perpetua was a
widow, since she released her infant son into the care of her mother,
though the child was brought to her regularly for nursing, and since
apparently her death would make the child an orphan. Perpetua's
two surviving brothers (a third had died as a child) were believers,
as was her mother; but her father was a pagan. He loved Perpetua
more than all his other children and made several attempts to persuade her to recant or deny her Christian faith in order to spare
her life.

One day shortly after her imprisonment began Perpetua's father
visited her, appealing to her for the sake of her life and for that of
her nursing baby to renounce her faith. Pointing to a water-pot or
some other container, Perpetua asked her father, "Can that vessel,
which you see, change its name?" When he answered that it could
not, Perpetua said to him, "Nor can I call myself any other than I
am, that is to say, a Christian."[1]

On another occasion as Perpetua's trial before the Roman procurator approached, her father tried again. In Perpetua's own words:

My father came over from the city worn out with exhaustion, and he went up to me in order to deflect me, saying: "My daughter, have pity on my white hairs! Show some compassion to your father, if I deserve to be called father by you. … Do not bring me into disgrace in all men's eyes! Look at your brothers, look at your mother and your aunt— look at your son, who won't be able to live if you die. Don't flaunt your insistence, or you'll destroy us all: for if anything happens to you, none of us will ever be able to speak freely and openly again."

This is what my father said, out of devotion to me, kissing my hands and flinging himself at my feet; and amid his tears he called me not "daughter" but "domina" [my lady]. And I grieved for my father's condition—for he alone of all my family would not gain joy from my ordeal. And I comforted him, saying: "At the tribunal things will go as God wills: for you must know that we are no longer in our own hands, but in God's." And he left me griefstricken.[2]

As Perpetua stood before Hilarian, the procurator of the province, her father made a final attempt. Apparently, Perpetua was the last of the prisoners to be examined because she records that all those who were questioned ahead of her boldly confessed Jesus Christ. When it was her turn, her father suddenly appeared, carrying her infant son. He appealed to her motherly instinct, begging her to consider the misery that she would bring on her son if she persisted. Even the judge, Hilarian, joined in, saying, "What! Will neither the gray hairs of a father you are going to make miserable, nor the tender innocence of a child, which your death will leave an orphan, move you? Sacrifice for the prosperity of the emperor."

Perpetua replied, "I will not do it."

Hilarian asked her directly, "Are you then a Christian?"

"Yes, I am," she replied.

After this exchange, the judge sentenced Perpetua and all her companions to be exposed to wild beasts at the emperor's festival games.[3]

There are several remarkable things about Perpetua and her martyrdom that can encourage us. First, the existing account of her imprisonment, trial, and death is regarded as reliably historical (as compared to some other martyr accounts that contain much legend) and is one of the earliest historical accounts of Christianity after the close of the New Testament. The fact that much of the story was written by Perpetua herself makes it one of the earliest pieces of writing by a Christian woman. The story was so highly regarded that it was read widely in African churches for the next several centuries and was treated as almost equivalent to Scripture.

Perpetua faced her martyrdom with a confidence and courage that did not come strictly from within herself, but was given to her by the Lord whom she so faithfully gave witness to. Her experience is full of evidence of how Christ sustained her and the others throughout their ordeal. He never abandoned them but remained close to them. They drew constant strength from His presence.

Jesus is the same yesterday, today, and forever, and what He did for them He will do for us (see Hebrews 13:8). He has promised never to leave us or forsake us (see Hebrews 13:5). Perpetua's courage inspires us even more when we remember that she and all the others, with the possible exception of one believer called Saturus, were *new* believers; it was only after they were in prison that they received baptism. They were in the early stages of learning the doctrines and disciplines of the faith.

This shows us that what counts ultimately is our commitment to Christ, not knowledge. Knowledge of our faith is very important, but knowledge alone does not give us the courage to stand firm. That comes only through the person and presence of Jesus Christ in our lives.

Essentially, Perpetua was no different from any of us. She was an ordinary woman who trusted Christ completely and was given the courage and confidence to be faithful unto death. As we learn to trust Christ, we will find that He gives us the courage and confidence as well to meet whatever challenges come our way.

Maybe you aren't called to be a martyr for your faith, but you are called to die to self. It takes courage to die! May we learn how to gain strength for the journey from the example of this legend from church history—Perpetua, faithful unto death.

Reflect & Pray

1. What in your life can unintentionally come between you and your relationship with Jesus Christ?
2. Perpetua identified herself as a Christian—not a daughter, a woman, or a mother. What is your identity tied to? Your career, family, church? What happens when you identify yourself with anything other than your faith in Jesus?
3. Do you think it would be easier to take a stand for Christ as a new believer or as one who has matured? Why or why not?
4. In what ways has Christ strengthened your faith and made you more courageous?

Dear God Almighty, if I were asked to renounce my faith today, I pray that you would give me the courage to refuse to deny Jesus Christ. May I stand strong and stand firm on your Word—the living Word. In Jesus' name, amen.

I Met God:
Sojourner Truth (1797–1883)

I will give thanks and praise to You,
for I am fearfully and wonderfully made;
Wonderful are Your works,
And my soul knows it very well.
My frame was not hidden from You,
When I was being formed in secret,
And intricately and skillfully formed [as if embroidered
with many colors] in the depths of the earth.
Your eyes have seen my unformed substance;
And in Your book were all written
The days that were appointed for me,
When as yet there was not one of them [even taking shape].

PSALM 139:14–16

Named Isabella by her parents but called "Belle," Sojourner Truth was born to a slave couple on a farm in upstate New York around 1797. From the beginning, her parents instilled in her the importance and value of hard work even amidst their enslaved conditions. Belle's mother also taught her to pray to God during times of trouble. Belle learned both lessons well even though she didn't think about God very much while she was growing up and, as a slave, had little opportunity to learn about Him.

By the time she was in her mid-twenties, Belle had belonged to five different slaveholders. She had married another slave named Tom and had given birth to five children. In 1824 Belle heard the news that the New York state legislature had passed a law abolishing slavery in the state. Under the terms of the law she and Tom would become free on July 4, 1827. In 1825, John Dumont, Belle's owner of fifteen years, was impressed with her hard work and offered her a deal: If she worked extra hard for the next year, he would free her and Tom a year early. Belle accepted eagerly and did her part. At the end of the year, however, a poor harvest caused Dumont to feel he could not afford to free them as he had promised. Feeling betrayed, Belle determined to run away, even though by law she would be free in another year.

Belle wondered when to make her attempt. Running away during the day would be foolish, and she was afraid of the dark. As her mother had taught her, Belle prayed to God, and He showed her what to do: leave around dawn, while everyone else was still asleep but there was enough light to see. Taking her youngest child, Sophia, Belle fled to the home of a Quaker couple a few miles away who gave them shelter. When Dumont found them there the next day, Belle refused to return. The Quaker couple bought her and Sophia from Dumont for $25 and then promptly set them free.

Belle looked forward to the day when all her family would be free. But before that day arrived, Dumont sold her only son. While walking home one day, Belle cried out to Jesus to intercede for her before the throne of God. Her prayer was answered when she met a perfect stranger on the road who asked her if her son had been returned yet. When she said no, the stranger pointed to a nearby house and told her that an attorney lived there who could help her. Belle went to see him, and within twenty-four hours the court had returned Peter to her. For the rest of her life Belle testified that she was certain that the stranger she had met on the road was sent from God to help her.[1]

For years before her freedom Belle had prayed to God for help in becoming free, promising that if He helped her, she would try to be good and remember to pray. Once she was free, however, she forgot about God. Then, on a festival day, John Dumont brought a wagon and invited Belle to visit her family on his farm. Years later, Sojourner Truth described the event to Harriet Beecher Stowe, the author of *Uncle Tom's Cabin*, who wrote it down:

Well, jest as I was goin' out to git into the wagon, I met God! An' says I, "O God, I didn't know as you was so great!" An' I turned right round an' come into the house, an' set down in my room; for 'twas God all around me. I could feel it burnin', burnin', burnin' all around me, an' goin' through me; an' I saw I was so wicked, it seemed as ef it would burn me up. An' I said, "O some-body, somebody, stand between God an' me! For it burns me!"

Then, honey, when I said so, I felt as it were somethin' like an amberill [umbrella] that came between me an' the light, an' I felt it was Somebody—Somebody that stood between me an' God; an' it felt cool, like a shade; an' says I, "Who's this that stands between me an' God?" … I begun to feel 'twas Somebody that loved me; an' I tried to know Him. … An' finally somethin' spoke out in me an' said, "This is Jesus!" An' I spoke out with all my might, an' says I, "This is Jesus! Glory be to God!" An' then the whole world grew bright, an' the trees they waved an' waved in glory, an' every little bit o' stone on the ground shone like glass; an' I shouted an' said, "Praise, praise, praise to the Lord!" An' I begun to feel such a love in my soul as I never felt before—love to all creatures. An' then, all of a sudden, it stopped, an' I said, "Dar's de white folks, that have abused you an' beat you an' abused your people—think o' them!" But then there came another rush of love through my soul, an' I cried out loud,

"Lord, Lord, I can love *even de white folks!*" … I jes' walked round an' round in a dream. Jesus loved me! I knowed it—I felt it. Jesus was my Jesus.[2]

Bell's conversion to Christ made a profound impact on her. Almost immediately she began preaching and talking about Jesus every chance she got. She took her children to church regularly and became very involved in the African Methodist Episcopal (AME) church.[3]

After many years in New York City, Bell felt God leading her to become an itinerant evangelist, going wherever He led her and depending on His providence to care for her needs. She already had a reputation as a powerful, forceful, and convincing preacher in her church; now God wanted her to step out and preach to others.

Sojourner Truth spent more than fifty years on the front lines, and God sustained her and guided her steps. He never changes in nature, purpose, or character. As He guided and sustained Sojourner Truth, so He will guide and sustain you as you trust Him and follow Him. The same courage He gave to her He will give to you. Believe Him and claim His promise!

Reflect & Pray

1. The words *slavery* and *racism* stir emotions. In some parts of the world, people continue to be judged by the color of their skin. Write what you think God's views are about this type of judgment. What Scriptures confirm this position?

2. Do you believe the statement that God created all people equal? Why or why not?

3. Have you ever felt discriminated against because of something that was beyond your control? What was your reaction? Would it be the same today?

4. Have you witnessed someone being unjustly treated? Did you step in and help? Would you today?

Dear heavenly Father, please instruct me about the right way to handle issues of racism. Help me realize that there is no one-size-fits-all solution to eliminating racism and that I must take action to correct the wrongs done to others. In Jesus' name, amen.

The Moses of Her People: Harriet Tubman (1820-1913)

> Then God also said to Moses, "This is what you shall say
> to the Israelites, 'The LORD, the God of your fathers, the God
> of Abraham, the God of Isaac, and the God of Jacob (Israel),
> has sent me to you.' This is My Name forever, and this
> is My memorial [name] to all generations.

EXODUS 3:15

*H*arriet Tubman was born as a slave in Maryland before the Civil War, and she was severely abused by her slaveholders as a child. By the time she reached adulthood her hatred of slavery had made her determined to be free at any cost, while her faith in God had instilled in her a confidence in her success and a fearlessness regarding her own personal safety. Those who saw Harriet in action during her years of personally leading slaves to freedom were impressed by the fact that she displayed absolutely no fear for herself while taking every care to protect the runaways she was responsible for. She believed implicitly that God was directing her steps and protecting her and that she would be taken only when and if God willed it. As Harriet herself expressed it to friends years later, "There are two things I have a right to, liberty or death. If I can't have one, I will have the other. For no man will take me alive. I will fight for my liberty as long as my strength lasts, and when the time comes for me to go, the Lord will let them take me."[1]

When she was twenty-five years old, Harriet married John Tubman, a free black. John had been born free and therefore had never known what slavery was like. He had a difficult time understanding Harriet's burning desire to be free. When Harriet made the decision to run away, she could not persuade John to come north with her. She determined to go alone, carrying a slip of paper bearing the name of someone who would help her.

The moment she walked across the state line into Pennsylvania, Harriet was overwhelmed with joy. For the first time in her life she was free! Years later she described the feeling: "I looked at my hands to see if I was the same person now I was free. Dere was such a glory trou de trees and ober de fields, and I felt like I was in heaven."[2]

She made her way to Philadelphia where she found work as a cook and maid at a hotel. She also found an inexpensive place to rent and began enjoying life as a free woman. Her heart was burdened, however, at the thought of her family—her brothers and sisters and her aging parents—still in bondage. She resolved within herself that with the Lord's help she would see all of them to freedom.

Harriet talked to God constantly, and He spoke to her in answer to her prayers and through dreams and visions. As a child of thirteen, Harriet had been severely injured when a plantation overseer, trying to stop a fleeing slave, had thrown an iron weight at him. Instead of hitting the man, the weight hit Harriet squarely on the forehead, crushing in the front of her skull. For weeks she lingered at the point of death, in and out of consciousness. It took her months to recover. After this, she began to have vivid, even prophetic, dreams. For the rest of her life Harriet also suffered periodic attacks of narcolepsy—she would suddenly fall asleep in the middle of whatever she was saying or doing, sleep for a few minutes, then wake up, picking up where she had left off as though nothing had happened.

In 1851, Harriet made a trip into Maryland to lead James, her oldest brother, to freedom. James and two friends left with Harriet in the middle of the night. Unfortunately, their escape was discovered very early and they were quickly pursued by blood-hounds and men on horseback. It seemed that only a miracle could save them. As they ran through the woods, Harriet heard a voice inside warning her of danger ahead. She turned to the left and the men followed, only to find their way blocked by a river. Harriet's voice told her to cross the river. Without hesitation, she plunged in and began wading to the other side. The water rose to her waist, then to her shoulders, then to her chin. Then it got shallower again until she reached the other side. The three men with her had hesitated at first, then plunged in after her with their pursuers close behind them in the woods.

The four of them soon came to a cabin where a family of free blacks lived. There they received shelter and food. Later Harriet learned that just ahead of them, before they had crossed the river, posters had been placed advertising rewards for their capture and officers had been waiting for them.[3]

Had Harriet not listened to the voice inside her, she and her charges would surely have been captured. This is just one example of the divine guidance and providence that sustained Harriet and helped her succeed against incredible odds.

After the war she returned to Auburn and married Nelson Davis, a black soldier she had met during the war, and she became involved in the women's suffrage movement. (Her first husband, who had stayed in Maryland, had also remarried.) She always opened her home to any who were in need—particularly blacks—and was so generous with what resources she had that she struggled all her life to have enough money for her own needs. In her later years, she established on her property a home for aged and impoverished blacks.

Eventually, Harriet deeded the property and the home to the AME Zion Church with which she was actively involved during her years in Auburn. Harriet Tubman died on March 10, 1913, greatly admired and respected for her courage, service, and high Christian and moral character. She was given a military funeral. Harriet Tubman's life is a testimony to what a person can do who learns to listen to God's voice and obey without question.

Because she trusted not in herself but in Him, she found His courage, strength, wisdom, insight, and protection available to her. Those same resources are ours as well if we will trust God and not depend on ourselves.

Let's also listen and obey the Spirit's voice. Who knows? Maybe you too will be added to the hall of heroes and heroines of courage as God enables you to proclaim, "Let my people go!"

Pioneers always blaze a trail for others to later walk.

Reflect & Pray

1. Have you ever encountered people who were being disenfranchised—at work, at school, or even at church? What might be your role in a situation like that?
2. Divine guidance and providence sustained Harriet and helped her succeed against incredible odds. How is that Source available for you today?
3. You may not have bloodhounds nipping at your heels as you run from those who wish you harm, but the evil one is chasing you to devour you. How can listening to God's voice help direct your paths?
4. Harriet's goal was to help as many slaves as possible. What goal keeps you focused and motivated?

Dear Lord, may I keep focused on you and your destiny for me, for when I am, nothing can harm me. Please give me the right goals to achieve that will establish your kingdom on earth as it is in heaven. In Jesus' name, amen.

Day 8

Overcoming Challenges:
Aimee Semple McPherson (1890-1944)

Therefore we do not become discouraged [spiritless,
disappointed, or afraid]. Though our outer self is
[progressively] wasting away, yet our inner self is being
[progressively] renewed day by day.

2 CORINTHIANS 4:16

In 1919 Aimee Semple McPherson and her children settled in Los Angeles, California, the city that would be her home for the rest of her life and that she would use as a base for her itinerant evangelism. She always called her house on Orange Grove Drive in Los Angeles the "House That God Built" because the land, the house, its furnishings, and the landscaping—all just a half block away from a school for her children—had been donated to her by people attending her meetings.[1]

Unlike many other evangelists of the time who stressed "hell-fire and brimstone," Aimee focused on a message of love and acceptance. This was undoubtedly one of the major reasons for her enormous appeal. Aimee's message was, in her own words, "the simple story of Jesus' love, and the outpoured Holy Spirit who has come to convict us of sin and draw us to the cross of Calvary, where, as we confess our sin, Jesus … cleanseth us from all unrighteousness."[2]

She believed that the secret of her success was her emphasis on Christ. Originally scheduled for two weeks, the meetings were extended twice. Even after five weeks there was no ebb in the tide of people coming for prayer, especially prayer for healing. Aimee tried at first to pray personally for as many as possible, but the demand was too great. In response to the overwhelming need, two outdoor healing services were scheduled in Balboa Park. San Diego police, augmented by U.S. Marines and U.S. Army personnel, handled traffic and crowd control. A Salvation Army band, an orchestra, and a large combined choir were on hand. Aimee also depended on a group of local ministers present to assist in anointing the sick with oil, the laying on of hands, and praying for healing.[3] As many as 30,000 people crowded into the park.

On January 1, 1923, Aimee Semple McPherson dedicated the Angelus Temple, the church building in Los Angeles that would become the hub of the wide-ranging ministries of her Echo Park Evangelistic Association. The full, or official, name of the church was the International Church of the Foursquare Gospel. The name "foursquare" referred to a four-point theme or emphasis that had become the doctrinal core of Aimee's preaching. It clearly illustrated the Christ-centered focus of her message: Jesus Christ as Savior, Healer, Baptizer in the Holy Spirit, and coming King.[4]

From the outset, Angelus Temple was one of the largest churches in Los Angeles. Its 5,300-seat sanctuary was filled to capacity regularly. The large platform area was built on hydraulic pistons so it could be raised or lowered to accommodate the needs of Aimee's illustrated sermons. A full schedule of services of different types and for different age groups kept the church open seven days a week. Her message was so simple and straightforward, her style so warm, her methods so innovative, that she attracted a wide and diverse audience: Hollywood actors and actresses, politicians, common folk, African Americans, and even members of the Ku Klux Klan.

The various ministries of the Temple have always been very practical in focus, seeking to meet human needs in any form. The

Temple commissary provided for the needs of thousands of poor and destitute people in the Los Angeles area. Other ministries extended help to women in trouble, alcoholics, prostitutes, and the uneducated. From its beginning and for decades after Aimee's death, the Prayer Tower operated around the clock, twenty-four hours a day, every day of the year.

Each of these ministries was a reflection of the heart of the woman who inspired them. Aimee genuinely loved people. She reached out personally to them wherever she went, often laboring far into the night to minister to them. People everywhere responded to and loved her for her compassion. Her heart for people also made her bold. She did not hesitate to go into a city's "red-light district" to talk with the prostitutes, to love them and share Jesus with them, and to invite them to her meetings. In San Diego in 1921, Aimee appeared between rounds at a boxing match to challenge those attending to find the "worst sinner in the city" and bring that person with them to the meeting the next night, where she promised to "go into the ring for Jesus."[5]

Aimee had a pioneering spirit and a vision for the future. This is revealed by the fact that in 1924 radio station KFSG began broadcasting, making Angelus Temple one of the first churches in the country to own and operate its own radio transmission facility. Aimee Semple McPherson was also the first woman in America to own a radio broadcasting license and was one of the first women to preach over the radio. Another sign of her far-reaching vision was her establishment of a training institute for ministers and other Christian workers. The institute was named LIFE: The Lighthouse of International Foursquare Evangelism. Through the years, this school has trained thousands of people for Christian ministry.

When Aimee Semple McPherson died in 1944, she left behind

a remarkable record of accomplishments. The denomination she founded still flourishes today with hundreds of churches and thousands of members worldwide. The Angelus Temple in Los Angeles still serves as the headquarters for the denomination and still conducts services to capacity crowds.

Aimee was the most well-known and popular evangelist of her day. During her life she personally baptized over 100,000 people. Although she is known by many for her healing ministry, her first priority was evangelism—winning people to saving faith in Jesus Christ. Healing was a vital part of what she called "full-gospel evangelism," but preaching Christ to save sinners was foremost.

Aimee Semple McPherson was a woman of courage. She overcame the grief and trauma of early widowhood and the stigma of divorce and built a powerful and effective ministry. In a society that still placed significant social and public restrictions on women, Aimee prevailed against significant odds: the prejudice against female ministers, the belief that women were not capable of succeeding without male guidance, and the belief that women did not have the ability to head large "business" organizations.

Reflect & Pray

1. Do you think female pastors have a place in today's churches? Why or why not?

2. Do you know someone who openly or subtly discriminates against a female leader? What do you think their motivation is? Do you agree or disagree with them? Why?

3. List a few women in the Bible who were used by God.

4. Do you think that women are as business-savvy as men? As spiritual? Why or why not?

Dear God, thank you for raising up women who listen to your voice and are determined to take action according to your Word. May I hear you and take action today. In Jesus' name, amen.

Day 9

The Peace of Jerusalem: Lydia Prince (1890–1975)

> But for now, I am going to Jerusalem to serve
> the saints (Jewish believers).
>
> ROMANS 15:25

*B*orn into a well-to-do Danish family, Lydia Christensen was the youngest of three children and the only one still unmarried. While at home with her family over the holiday break, Lydia discussed her yearnings with her mother. The elder woman felt that what Lydia was missing was a home and children of her own. Although Lydia couldn't explain how she felt, she knew it was deeper than that. Fumbling for the right words, Lydia told her mother, "If there was something special in life that another woman wouldn't do—even if it was difficult or dangerous—that's what I'd like to do!"

Determined to find an answer to her inner restlessness, she gave her housekeeper the week off in order to spend the time completely alone. Bypassing the books of philosophy and literature on her shelf, Lydia pulled down the Bible that she hadn't read since her college days. She opened it to the book of Matthew and began reading. The Beatitudes in chapter 5 spoke to her heart, especially the words, "Blessed are they which do hunger and thirst after righteousness: for they shall be filled" (Matthew 5:6 KJV). Hungry and thirsty were just how she felt. Reading further, she was particularly arrested by Jesus' words in chapter 7:

> Ask, and it shall be given you; seek, and ye shall find; knock,
> and it shall be opened unto you: for every one that asketh

receiveth; and he that seeketh findeth; and to him that knocketh it shall be opened. … Enter ye in at the strait gate: for wide is the gate, and broad is the way, that leadeth to destruction, and many there be which go in thereat: because strait is the gate, and narrow is the way, which leadeth unto life, and few there be that find it. (Matthew 7:7–8, 13–14 KJV)

Lydia gave her life fully to Jesus and began to feel called to move to the Holy Land. She resigned her teaching job, moved to Jerusalem, and began to live by faith. Her life in Jerusalem became a wonderful example of a life truly lived by faith. She left behind all she had known and, like Abram centuries before, traveled to an unknown land simply by God's direction. Her circumstances demanded complete trust in God for the provision of every need. Time after time her resources ran low, only to be replenished by the unexpected arrival of letters or cards containing gifts of money. Some came from her mother, some from her former colleagues at the school where she had taught, some from other friends she knew. Some of the gifts were anonymous. Whatever the source, Lydia continually found her needs met by a bountiful and faithful God. Lydia's absolute faith in God also gave her courage. She endured much hardship, privation, hunger, thirst, and even physical danger in a city and land torn by the centuries-old hostilities and strife between Jews and Arabs. She came to understand that her calling was not only to care for the homeless children of the city, but also to intercede in prayer, to pray continually for the peace of Jerusalem.

Lydia lived in Jerusalem for more than twenty years, becoming "Mama" to scores of Arab and Jewish children she kept and loved and cared for in her home. In 1945 she met Derek Prince, a British soldier stationed in Jerusalem. At this time Lydia's "family" consisted of eight girls: six were Jewish, one was a Palestinian Arab, and one was English.[1]

Derek had become a Christian several years before in the early days of World War II. After the war, he took his discharge in Jerusalem, entered full-time Christian ministry, and married Lydia. They remained in Jerusalem until 1948, witnessing the rebirth of the nation of Israel and enduring the new nation's war for independence.[2]

After leaving Israel, Lydia and Derek labored faithfully together through thirty years of marriage in Christian service that went from pastoring churches to a large and expanding international ministry. Lydia died suddenly of heart failure in 1975. She was in her mid-eighties.

Lydia Prince left behind a legacy of countless lives changed by the power of God and the living Christ. This is particularly true for those children who lived with her during her years in Jerusalem. Another, perhaps even more important legacy is her heart for Jerusalem and its people and her insight into God's plan for Israel, gained through many years of faithful prayer and loving service. This insight is best understood in Lydia's own words from a letter she wrote to her mother:

> You ask what you can do to help … We Christians have a debt that has gone unpaid for many centuries—to Israel and to Jerusalem. It is to them that we owe the Bible, the prophets, the apostles, the Savior Himself. For far too long we have forgotten this debt, but now the time has come for us to begin repaying it—and there are two ways that we can do this.
>
> First, we need to repent of our sins against Israel: at best, our lack of gratitude and concern; at worst, our open contempt and persecution.

Then, out of true love and concern, we must pray as the psalmist tells us, "for the peace of Jerusalem," remembering that peace can only come to Jerusalem as Israel turns back to God.[3]

Perhaps you too are to be a burden-bearer for Jesus, taking up your cross through missionary endeavors. Is He knocking on your heart to be an intercessor for Israel? My suggestion is to just say, "Yes!" Surrender now to your appointment with the Jewish people by sharing the love of Yeshua. Say yes!

Reflect & Pray

1. Many times we get comfortable in our own little corners of the world and don't venture out past our current surroundings. Have you ever felt there was "more" than the life you're leading right now?
2. Is God calling you to be a missionary in a faraway land? Why or why not?
3. Can you be a missionary without moving away from your current home? How?
4. What steps can you take today to become a voice in your own community for the gospel?

Heavenly Father, please give me the courage to take action concerning my role in spreading the gospel of Jesus Christ. I place all my trust in you to provide opportunities where I can share your love with others. In Jesus' name, amen.

Day 10

Prelude to Revival:
Bertha Smith (1888–1988)

The power of God caused the word to spread,
and the people were greatly impacted.

ACTS 19:20

*W*hen Bertha Smith first arrived in China as a missionary she became concerned very quickly about the low level of spirituality and commitment among Chinese believers. This burden was shared by the other missionaries.[1]

They believed that a genuine revival was the only answer. Their conviction about this was strengthened as many of the missionaries experienced personal revivals in their own lives. God was moving in the Shantung province of China, preparing the land for a great outpouring of the Holy Spirit. He began by working in the hearts and lives of the missionaries.

During the summer months, the missionaries had opportunities to attend annual conferences on various themes related to the spiritual life. These conferences were characterized by dynamic speakers and teachers and a powerful moving of the Holy Spirit to such a degree that many of the missionaries received deep refreshing and significant spiritual renewal. Bertha was one of these. The most significant change for her was learning the secret to consistent victory in her Christian life, to victory over her "old self." The key was in not trying to *overcome* the flesh—an impossible task. Rather, it was in regarding it as *dead*—crucified with Christ. She realized that she had been wrongly struggling to crucify herself, rather than considering her flesh already dead in Christ.[2]

It was the truth that Paul taught the Romans when he wrote, "Likewise reckon ye also yourselves to be dead indeed unto sin, but alive unto God through Jesus Christ our Lord" (Romans 6:11 KJV). Bertha explained the truth this way: "You cannot consecrate the old sinful self to God; you assign it to death."[3]

Bertha and the other missionaries felt an increasing burden from the Lord to pray for revival in China. This became so intense that they set aside the first day of each month for that specific purpose. They maintained this practice faithfully for several years before revival came. This committed, consistent discipline of prayer was one of the catalysts for the great revival that swept across the Shantung province, and indeed all of China, in 1927.

Another catalyst in the revival was an evangelical Lutheran missionary from Norway named Marie Monsen. God used this deeply spiritual woman to spark revival fires wherever she went. In March 1927, she fled to the Chinese port city of Chefoo to escape political unrest farther inland. Many other missionaries had taken temporary refuge in Chefoo also. Among them were Bertha and the other Southern Baptist missionaries whom she worked with. They invited Marie Monsen to share her testimony with them. Marie told of her experiences in Bible teaching and evangelism in the field and also of the many instances she had seen of sick people being healed by the grace of God. The testimony of divine healing was a new and unusual concept for the Baptist missionaries, yet they were profoundly moved and touched by Marie Monsen's words.[4]

If any single event can be said to be the "beginning" of the Shantung revival, it was the powerful prayer meeting in March 1927 which involved Marie Monsen and the Baptist missionaries. The Holy Spirit inspired brokenness and deep confession of personal sin on the part of the missionaries. They resolved differences between one another and there was great cleansing of their lives and hearts. The primary purpose of the prayer meeting was to pray for the physical healing of Mrs. Ola Culpepper, Dr. Culpepper's wife, who had suffered for many years from optic neuritis—the decay of the optic nerve. It was a painful and degenerative condition.

Although she was slowly going blind, Mrs. Culpepper could still see relatively well with glasses. After the time of confession and cleansing, the missionaries laid hands on Mrs. Culpepper and prayed for her. The Spirit was so strong that when two Chinese cooks who worked at the mission and who had great animosity toward each other walked into the room, they were immediately brought under deep conviction. They confessed their sins to each other and accepted Christ as their Savior on the spot. After this Mrs. Culpepper testified that her pain was completely gone. It never returned. Although the vision in her most severely damaged eye was not completely restored, her vision in both eyes improved significantly and permanently.[5]

Although everyone in the group was rejoicing at the goodness and grace of God, Bertha suddenly felt convicted by their behavior. She told the others how inconsistent it seemed to spend so much time in confession, soul-searching, and prayer for each other when they had never done so in order to pray for the spiritual awakening of the Chinese people. Bertha's words hit the group like a thunderclap. As Bertha described it:

> Our mountaintop of ecstasy suddenly became a valley of humiliation. We all went to our knees in contrite confession for having been so careless as to have gone along supposing that we were right with the Lord, while holding all kinds of attitudes which could have kept the Lord's living water from flowing through us to the Chinese.[6]

Bertha's experiences in China both before and during the Shantung revival set the tone and pattern for the rest of her life. Once she understood the principles of dying to self and how to be filled with the Spirit on a continuing basis, her life was never again the same. The secret was to keep her "sins confessed up to date." It was important to keep a short sin account before God—to confess and renounce sin as soon as the Holy Spirit revealed it to her. This is the same principle that she taught countless believers through the remaining years of her life.

The secret of Bertha Smith's courage and effectiveness throughout a century-long life is that she learned how to die to self: to regard herself as being dead to sin but alive to God through Jesus Christ (see Romans 6:11). That is the key to spiritual victory, to personal revival, and to effectiveness in ministry. Bertha Smith lived her life with spiritual courage and holy boldness because, like the apostle Paul, she knew that "For to me, to live is Christ [He is my source of joy, my reason to live] and to die is gain [for I will be with Him in eternity]" (Philippians 1:21).

Reflect & Pray

1. How did God use these women in China to bring change to people who had never heard of salvation through Jesus Christ?

2. Why do you think Communist nations are prohibitive about allowing missionaries to share the gospel with their people?

3. How has the situation changed in China from the time Bertha Smith was there until today?

4. What can you do to help people in countries who have never heard of the living God?

Dear living God of heaven and earth, I pray that you will open doors and windows of opportunity for me to witness in any way possible to people who desperately need to hear of your love, mercy, grace, and faithfulness. Thank you. In Jesus' name, amen.

Day 11

Saving God's People:
Corrie ten Boom (1892–1983)

> Now therefore, if you will in fact obey My voice
> and keep My covenant (agreement), then you shall be
> My own special possession *and* treasure from among all
> peoples [of the world], for all the earth is Mine.
>
> EXODUS 19:5

During World War II, Corrie ten Boom, a fifty-year-old unmarried Dutch watchmaker, and other members of her family put their lives on the line to harbor and assist frightened people who had become enemies of the state for no other reason than that they were Jews. In defiance of the repressive Nazi government that occupied their beloved Holland, the ten Booms hid fugitive Jews in their home and helped them escape to freedom. By the time it was all over, Corrie's father, her oldest sister, and a nephew had died in concentration camps. Other family members spent time in jail, and Corrie herself survived ten months of imprisonment—first in a Dutch prison, then in a concentration camp in Holland, and finally in the infamous Ravensbrück camp in Germany, where 96,000 women died.

From all external appearances, there was very little about Corrie during the first fifty years of her life that would lead anyone to expect that she would ever become involved in such dangerous activities. She lived all those years in the same house where she was born: an ancient structure known as the Beje that housed her father's watch and clock shop on the first floor and the family's living quarters on the floors above. Like her oldest sister Betsie, Corrie helped her father in the watch shop. She took such an interest in the work that she eventually became the first licensed woman watchmaker in Holland. Corrie and her family were regular, active members of the Dutch Reformed Church. These early years were characterized by a regular, comfortable routine to everyday life. Yet within this familiar sameness of day-to-day life, God was preparing Corrie and her family for the great acts of courage and devotion that they would be called upon to perform during the years of Nazi oppression.

On February 28, 1944, after about eighteen months of underground activity, the inevitable happened: the Beje was raided. The ten Booms had been betrayed by a Dutch man working for the Nazis who had posed as a Jew needing help. During the raid, Corrie, Betsie, and their father were arrested, along with numerous others who appeared at the Beje, unaware that anything was wrong. The seven Jews sheltered there were not discovered, however. They had made it into the secret room in Corrie's bedroom. After several days in hiding, they were able to escape to safety.

It was the family's faith and confidence in God's protection that would sustain them through the horrors that lay ahead. The next day the prisoners were transported to a Dutch prison in the coastal town of Scheveningen. There Corrie and Betsie were held for several months. While in prison they received word that the others taken in the raid at the Beje had been released after a few weeks. They eventually learned that their father, who was well into his eighties, had died after only ten days in prison.

In the late spring of 1944, Betsie and Corrie were transferred to Vught, a concentration camp on Dutch soil. There, using a small Bible they had smuggled in with them, Corrie and Betsie held secret prayer meetings in the barracks at night, sharing the light and hope of Jesus Christ with the other women.

As the Allied forces advanced after the invasion of Europe in

June 1944, the camp at Vught was evacuated. Corrie and Betsie and hundreds of others were transported by freight train to Ravensbruck, a larger and much more brutal camp in Germany. If any place could have earned the designation of hell on earth, it would have been Ravensbruck. Yet it was here, in the midst of the darkness of human sin and brutality, that the light of Christ shone brightly in the lives and witness of the ten Boom sisters.

After many months, Betsie died in the camp. Three days later, Corrie received her notice of discharge. Finally, on January 1, 1945, she walked out of Ravensbrück a free woman.[1]

During the remainder of her life, she influenced countless thousands, perhaps even millions, by the testimony of her life and her witness to God's faithfulness. As a "tramp for the Lord," Corrie sought God's direct guidance concerning where to go and how long to stay, trusting Him to provide for her every need. She never appealed for money or other kinds of financial support. This was part of her absolute trust in the God who had sustained her so absolutely throughout her life and particularly in Ravensbrück. Her courage came from a source beyond herself. It lay in the One for whom she had lived exclusively since the age of five, the One whom she had met daily in the pages of the Bible, the One to whom she prayed regularly. In all her years, she never found Him to fail. Corrie found courage because she knew that God is good and that God is faithful. He never puts on us more than we can bear. Whatever He requires of us, He equips us to do. Corrie walked with God, and in His strength bore the unbearable and prevailed to victory.

Reflect & Pray

1. Have you read or heard about what happened in the Nazi concentration camps? About Ravensbrück? What do you think about the injustices that occurred?

2. In what ways have you acted courageously on behalf of another like Corrie and her family did?

3. How have you seen God's power and strength working in your life?

4. Although now we are all God's children through the blood of Christ shed on the cross, Jews are still being persecuted worldwide. What might God be asking you to do to help their plight?

Dear Father in heaven, I thank you for the Jewish people and their special relationship with you. You are the Father of all and I want to honor all of your children. Please give me the courage to take action when I see injustices. In Jesus' name, amen.

Day 12

Turning Darkness into Light:
Jackie Pullinger

If we [freely] admit that we have sinned and confess our sins,
He is faithful and just [true to His own nature and promises],
and will forgive our sins and cleanse us continually from
all unrighteousness [our wrongdoing, everything not in
conformity with His will and purpose].

1 JOHN 1:9

Jackie Pullinger had talked about being a missionary since she was five years old, even though for many years she had no real idea what a missionary was. She'd had a conventional English upbringing—attending a boarding school and being confirmed in the Church of England. Higher education followed at the Royal College of Music, where Jackie studied piano and oboe.[1]

Upon completing her degree, she began a career teaching music. However, she could not escape the feeling that she needed to give her life to something. Although she had been confirmed in the Church of England, the Christian faith did not become real to Jackie until she was in college. She encountered a group of friends who obviously enjoyed their relationship with Jesus and could discuss their experience and feelings about it with ease and joy. This concept intrigued Jackie. She states:

This was the first time that I had met Christians who did not look unhappy, guilty or grim, and my music college Christian Union … had only served to confirm my worst fears and impressions of earnest organists trying to get to heaven. I preferred brass players. I avoided the Christians while unable to avoid the unhappy conviction that at some time God himself would nail me for my shortcomings and I would have to account for my life."[3]

God reawakened within Jackie her childhood dream of becoming a missionary, but she was a single woman and too young and unqualified to be accepted by any of the conventional missionary societies. Every door seemed shut, and she wondered if she had heard God correctly. Desperate for answers and direction, Jackie attended a special prayer meeting with friends, and there God spoke to her. He said, "Go. Trust Me, and I will lead you. I will instruct you and lead you in the way in which you shall go; I will guide you with My eye."

At that, Jackie knew that she must take action and obey. After much prayer and godly counsel, Jackie decided that God had doors to open for her that she had not yet seen. She decided to allow God to lead her directly and go on a daring adventure. She bought the cheapest boat ticket that she could find that stopped at the greatest number of countries and prayed for God's direction to know where to get off and how He wanted her to proceed from there.

So with this great act of faith, Jackie found herself stepping off a boat in Hong Kong in 1966 after traveling halfway around the globe. She had no missionary agency or organized support for her back in Britain, no job, and no contacts. She had very little money and no clear direction of what God had in store for her, but she had the assurance that God had called her and would continue to direct her.

She began to work within a six-acre enclave of Hong Kong known as the Walled City. One of its Chinese names is "Hak Nam," which means "darkness." Cramped, secluded, and filthy, the Walled

City was home to anywhere from 30,000 to 60,000 people—no one knew for sure how many—and it was a haven of opium dens, heroin huts, brothels, pornography theaters, illegal gambling, smuggling, and many other kinds of vice. Virtually ignored by the rest of Hong Kong, the Walled City was accessible only through dark, narrow alleys between shops located on its outer edges. There were no sanitary facilities—refuse and excrement were simply dumped out in the streets and alleys—and electricity was illegally tapped from supplies outside the City.[2]

Daily life in the Walled City was defined by a number of gangs who controlled all aspects of vice, extortion, and crime. The boundaries of each gang's territory were clearly defined, and violence between rival gangs was frequent. Gang membership provided a sense of family and acceptance that young Chinese men rarely found elsewhere in "Hak Nam." The city called "darkness" was in great need of the light of Jesus, and Jackie began trying to relate to the people she met there, seeking to share the light of Christ as she had opportunity.

Externally, the Walled City was one of the most revolting places on earth, yet every time she entered it, Jackie felt a profound sense of joy. This confirmed for her that she was where God had called her.[3]

Through Jackie's ministry in the Walled City over the years, hundreds of Chinese came to Christ: drug dealers, drug addicts, prostitutes, gang members, and gang bosses. In 1997, Hong Kong was turned over to the Chinese government. Yet lives continue to be changed throughout Asia as a result of the work Jackie began in the late 1960s. Jackie travels periodically to Britain and the United States to speak and to teach.

God was able to do a mighty work among the lost and outcast people of the Walled City in Hong Kong because a young

English woman had the faith to believe that He would lead her and the courage to act on that faith. Jackie entered Hong Kong with no human resources to fall back on. She had followed the Spirit's leading to Hong Kong and knew that she was totally dependent upon God for her protection, resources, and success. Her life is a testimony to the truth that there is no limit to what one person can accomplish when he or she commits him or herself completely into the hands of the Lord.

Reflect & Pray

1. How have you had to depend upon God to provide what you need? What was the outcome?

2. What doubts do you have that the Lord will give you the resources you need to accomplish His plan for your life?

3. What five Scripture verses confirm God is your provider? Write them in your own words.

4. What do you think of Jackie Pullinger's courage to confront criminals in a foreign land? What may God be asking you to confront courageously in your life?

Dear Provider of all that is good and righteous, thank you for giving me what I need to fulfill my potential and your destiny for me. I choose to honor you through living a holy life dedicated to furthering your kingdom on earth as it is in heaven. In Jesus' name, amen.

Day 13

You Are Chosen!

Therefore humble yourselves under the mighty hand of God
[set aside self-righteous pride], so that He may exalt you [to a
place of honor in His service] at the appropriate time, casting
all your cares [all your anxieties, all your worries, and all your
concerns, once and for all] on Him, for He cares about you
[with deepest affection, and watches over you very carefully].

1 PETER 5:6–7

*C*onsider for a moment the nine women whose lives have just been profiled. They are so different from each other in race, nationality, culture, background, and time in history. What is the common bond between them? What connects Joan of Arc, Vibia Perpetua, Sojourner Truth, Harriet Tubman, Aimee Semple McPherson, Lydia Prince, Bertha Smith, Corrie ten Boom, and Jackie Pullinger? Very simply, they were *ordinary women* who knew an *extraordinary God*. When they gave to Him their very ordinariness, when they came to Him in their human weakness, He showed Himself strong on their behalf and used them in extraordinary ways.

You may feel that you are the least qualified for God to use and the most unlikely candidate for His Spirit to fall upon. Guess what? You're just the kind of person He chooses! God makes a point of choosing the weak things of the world to shame the mighty and the foolish things of the world to shame the wise (see 1 Corinthians 1:27). God is revealed and glorified in your weakness. The apostle Paul himself knew this. He wrote to the Corinthians:

But He has said to me, "My grace is sufficient for you [My lovingkindness and My mercy are more than enough—always available—regardless of the situation]; for [My] power is being perfected [and is completed and shows itself most effectively] in [your] weakness." Therefore, I will all the more gladly boast in my weaknesses, so that the power of Christ [may completely enfold me and] may dwell in me. (2 Corinthians 12:9)

Do you fall into the category of the weak, the ordinary, the least likely? If you do, take heart! You are a prime target for the Lord to come and wrap Himself around you. Isn't that great news?

Years ago, I had a dream in which I was entering a large coliseum. It was in a foreign country and the king's court was about to convene. Every woman who entered the building was given a number. Mine was number twenty-nine. The king had not yet come out as I sat down to watch the proceedings. I ended up sitting next to a woman who simply despised me, no matter how hard I tried to be nice. For some reason I just irritated the daylights out of her. Anything nice I tried to do or say was like rubbing salt into a wound. She became extremely hostile to me and was constantly reviling me, putting cigarette ashes on my head and that kind of thing.

In this dream, during the preliminary proceedings prior to the king's appearance, someone was calling out the different numbers assigned to the women in the room. Whoever's number was called had to go spend the night with a man, whether or not she wanted to. The hateful woman next to me called out my number. I was so sickened at the thought of what I was supposed to do that I simply got up and ran out of the auditorium as fast as I could.

Unknown to me at the time, the king's son had come out and was going to choose his bride that day. He had heard my number called and had seen me run away. He put his fingers to his lips and said, "I like that. She ran away from evil. I choose *her!*" Everyone began looking around, saying, "Where is she? Where did she go?"

Suddenly I came back in the room dressed in regal robes. My face looked totally different. I knew it was me, but I didn't recognize myself. I approached the court and stood in front of the king's son. He kissed me and gave me a scepter. There were two thrones and we both turned around and sat down on them. That's how the dream ended.

I have come to understand since then that this dream wasn't just for me, but for all of us—the Bride of Christ. It is a dream of where the Lord wants to take us. We are His chosen ones, set apart before we were ever born. Paul told the Ephesians: "just as [in His love] He chose us in Christ [actually selected us for Himself as His own] before the foundation of the world, so that we would be holy [that is, consecrated, set apart for Him, purpose-driven] and blameless in His sight" (Ephesians 1:4).

For years I asked the Lord, "God, what's the deal about number twenty-nine? What does it mean?" He answered my question by showing me Scriptures such as: "'For I know the plans and thoughts that I have for you,' says the LORD, 'plans for peace and well-being and not for disaster, to give you a future and a hope.'" (Jeremiah 29:11); "But you are a chosen race, a royal priesthood, a consecrated nation, a [special] people for God's own possession, so that you may proclaim the excellencies [the wonderful deeds and virtues and perfections] of Him who called you out of darkness into His marvelous light" (1 Peter 2:9); Esther 2:9, where Esther is given the choice place in the king's harem; and Psalm 29, which talks about the voice of the Lord thundering, causing the deer to calf, stripping bare the forests, echoing across the waters, and breaking open the way. Then there is Acts 29. Now I know there is no chapter 29 to the book of Acts. *Because we're writing it through our lives as followers of Jesus.* That's what we're called to come into. We have been chosen. That's what the number twenty-nine means—*chosen.*

Each of us has a great responsibility to the generation that will follow us—our children. If they are to fully realize their place in God's plan, then we must give them a pure stream from which to drink—a stream unpolluted by bitterness, contention, division, unbelief, and fear, a stream where the way ahead has been cleared by pioneers and heroes who have gone before.

Reflect & Pray

1. How have you seen God use ordinary people to do extraordinary things? What do you have in common with the women you've read about so far?
2. Is there a dream that holds a special meaning to you? What Scriptures relate to that dream? Write them down.
3. List all the ways you are unique for the glory of God.
4. As a chosen heir of the King of kings, how can you make a difference in your family, community, state, and nation?

My dear King, thank you for the inheritance I received when Jesus died to redeem me from my sins. I pray that you will show me the righteous path to walk and that I will do so courageously and with the dignity afforded to all children of the Almighty God on high. In Jesus' name, amen.

Seize the Day

"So if you are not even able to do a very little thing [such as that], why are you worried about the rest? Consider the lilies and wildflowers, how they grow [in the open field]. They neither labor nor spin [wool to make clothing]; yet I tell you, not even Solomon in all his glory and splendor dressed himself like one of these. But if this is how God clothes the grass which is in the field today and tomorrow is thrown into the furnace, how much more will He clothe you? You of little faith!"

LUKE 12:26–28

The Word and the Spirit always agree. If the Holy Spirit is the One who both empowers you and releases you, then His Word is consistent with that. When you welcome a heroic anointing—when you welcome the call of God to be the heroic woman that you're called to be—then you welcome the responsibility to launch out, on the firmest biblical foundation possible, the generation that is rising.

How can you be sure to maintain an unpolluted stream to pass on to those who follow? It requires hard work, a lot of prayer, and constant vigilance. There are seven general principles that we all need to take to heart that will help us keep our stream pure.

1. *Develop a passion for God's Word.* First Peter says, "But in your hearts set apart Christ as Lord. Always be prepared to give an answer to everyone who asks you to give the reason for the hope that you have" (1 Peter 3:15 NIV). How important is the Bible in your daily Christian life? Do you read it devotionally and let it go at that? Do you study it vigorously, trying to understand everything

you can? Have you been hurt by the way others have used the Bible in the past to tie you down or hold you back and keep you from realizing God's call on your life? Because of this, have you distanced yourself from the Bible, telling yourself that you want to focus on being "spiritual" rather than biblical?

2. *Expect to be wounded.* David said to God, "For they persecute those you wound and talk about the pain of those you hurt" (Psalm 69:26 NIV). Have you ever been hurt because you were trying to stand up for Jesus? Do you carry deep pain over something that another person, even another Christian, said or did to you? Wounds are an occupational hazard for heroes. Whenever you accept the calling of God, whenever you stand up against the norm, you will be wounded. Wounds hurt. Sometimes they hurt very badly. Our theology of victory does not exempt us from bruises and wounds. God uses them to make us into the heroes that He has called us to be. Even if the wound comes from someone who is not in the Lord, the wound itself is something that God wants us to embrace redemptively.

Take courage! The pain is worth the price if it means you can pass on an untainted stream to those who come after you. Embracing the pain for the sake of others is part of being a hero.

3. *God wounds you to develop your character.* To many people today, character means not doing certain things. That's not what it means in the Bible, however. In the Scriptures, the word *character* means to bear up under suffering and difficulty. In Ruth 3:11, Ruth is called a woman of noble character because she bore up under difficulty.

God will use the hard things in your life to prepare you for the anointing that He wants to place upon you. The writer of Hebrews said of Jesus, "Although He was a son, He learned obedience from what He suffered" (Hebrews 5:8 NIV). Think of what Jesus suffered:

rejection by His family, the death of His earthly father, ridicule, crucifixion, and death. Through all this He learned obedience and thus became a source for His generation. In the same way the Lord uses the hardships of your life to build in you pillars of character that can sustain the anointing that will rest on them. God's anointing must work on you before it can work *through* you.

4. *Don't give place to bitterness.* The book of Hebrews says, "See to it that no one misses the grace of God and that no bitter root grows up to cause trouble and defile many" (12:15 NIV). The Greek word for "defile" carries the idea of a dye for coloring clothes. If you allow roots of bitterness to spring up in your life, they will dye or taint everything you do.

Have you ever heard someone speak where the words were great and the message solid, but there was something about his or her spirit that just didn't sit right with you? There may have been a root of bitterness or some other negative force that tainted the flow of their lives. Each of us as believers minister out of the flow of our spirits and out of the Holy Spirit in us. If we allow bitterness to dwell in our lives, we taint that flow and produce weakened, diseased fruit.

Any time we take offense at a wrong or a hurt, we open ourselves up to be trapped by the enemy. The Greek word in the New Testament for "offense" is *skandalon,* from which we get the word *scandal.* It literally refers to a trap-stick or snare—that part of an animal trap that sets off the trap when the animal steps into it. Our bitterness, our offense, can become the trigger that snares us in the enemy's trap.

What do you do about bitterness in your life? When the Israelites in the wilderness complained to Moses because the water was too bitter to drink, Moses threw a piece of wood into the water and the water became sweet (see Exodus 15:23–25 NIV). When you throw the wood (the cross of Jesus) onto your waters of bitterness, they will become sweet.

5. *Submit to one another.* A lot of us get uncomfortable with the words *submit* or *submission,* and with good reason. There is no doubt that, over the centuries, many men have treated women wrongly. There's also no question that many men have acted as though they could go it alone without the gifts that women could bring. The great danger that lies in the current release of women into ministry is that, unless the Holy Spirit is leading and is followed, this shift will degrade into a feministic Christian women's movement that is at odds with the men.

What God wants now is not an independent women's movement and an independent men's movement, but a *teaming up* that many men and women in the church don't yet understand. Submitting to one another out of reverence for Christ is the context for everything that follows.

6. *Don't compromise your call.* There is a tendency among Christian women today that when the traditional and normal corridors of power and ministry are closed to them, they seek alternative routes, especially the ones the men aren't interested in. Let's take intercession, for example. Frankly, most men aren't interested in intercession. There are many more women than men in the intercession ministry. Now, if that's your calling, get after it! Don't hesitate! As we walk in the character we're called to walk in and as His anointing rests upon us, He will break any yokes. Don't compromise the high call in your heart. The Lord will prepare the way.

7. *Drive a stake in the heart of the fear of man.* Quite often the fear of man stems from the fact that we have too lofty a picture of humanity and too limited a picture of God. Man and his institutions seem so big and substantial while our concept of God is restrained by sin and unbelief. But as you grow in your walk with

the Lord, as you learn to worship Him and behold His presence, as you cry out to Him, He will give you such a high view and a holy transforming vision of who Jesus is, and a high and transformed view of who you are and what you are called to be, that the opinions of men fade in comparison.

Reflect & Pray

1. Of the seven guidelines, which two hold more meaning to you than the others? Why?
2. Are you holding a bitter attitude toward anyone? How might this bitterness hold you back from receiving fully what God has for you?
3. How do you want to seize the day—practically in everyday life?
4. In what ways do you fear man (others)? Are these fears real or imagined? What steps can you take to overcome these fears?

Father, I surrender my life to the call to courage. Here I am. Change me. Use me. Drive fear out of me. I volunteer freely to be on the front lines in Jesus' name. Be glorified through my life. Amen!

Inner Quiet Prayer

In the same way the Spirit [comes to us and] helps us in
our weakness. We do not know what prayer to offer or how to
offer it as we should, but the Spirit Himself [knows our need
and at the right time] intercedes on our behalf with sighs
and groanings too deep for words.

ROMANS 8:26

*I*f we want to find God in our everyday experience and sense His
real presence throughout all life's struggles and joys, we must
learn about a kind of prayer few of us understand. I am speaking
about the prayer of inner quiet.

In the psalms, we discover long lists of God's amazing attributes
and His great and mighty acts. We read: "You are the God who does
wonders"; "You have demonstrated your power among the people";
and "With Your mighty arm You have redeemed Your people, the
sons of Jacob and Joseph." We get into the pace of those words,
imagining a God who is always on the move. Unfortunately, often
we miss the all-important instruction at the end: "selah." *Pause a
minute and calmly think about what you've just read.*

"Pause. Think about Me." In this tender instruction we hear the
echo of God's voice calling to us from out of time, calling us apart
to be alone with Him. Throughout our busy days, we run until we
drop and then get up the next day and start all over again.

Sadly, although we often complain about our demanding,
stressed-out lives, most of us have become accustomed to the
frantic pace. We scarcely know what to do with ourselves when
things slow down. Some of us are even afraid to slow down—afraid

because we know what will happen. We know that we've been running, running, running—keeping just ahead of the wind at our backs. And if we suddenly stop, the whirlwind of promises we've made and responsibilities we've picked up—everything that's swirling in our wake—will catch up with us. We've kept just a step ahead, but in a moment it could suddenly overtake us from behind. In truth, we have created these high-pressured lives, and still we ask, "Where did all these demands and all this stress come from?"

At the same time, we sense our own desire to retreat to the wonderful place in spirit, to enter the quiet sanctuary where God abides. We may even sense His call. But we become even more frustrated because of the seemingly increased demand someone is placing on us and our crammed schedules. Isn't that often our first objection when someone encourages us to give prayer a greater space in our lives? "I don't have the *time*." We give up in frustration before we even start, and we never answer God's love-call.

No matter how busy your lifestyle, no matter how stressed you've been, you can learn how to enter the secret place with God and know His real presence with you every day.

Be patient with yourself. Learning to change the lifestyle you've been living is going to take time. At the same time, you will also need to learn how to be patient waiting upon God. Although God is always present with us, coming into the secret place with Him is one thing you cannot hurry. You're not going to get there right away if you're a speed-reader, or if you're a great administrator who lives by a checklist. None of the things you know how to do to "make things happen" will help you come into this place in spirit.

No matter who you are, you'll only find your way to the secret place with God if you learn to take the time.

I can hear your objection: "I don't *have* time."

I assure you, I know all about the issue of time … and the lack thereof.

Some years ago, Jim came home on fire after being at a fantastic Christian conference. He could hardly sit down. He walked from room to room, reviewing all the amazing details. "God was so great!" He kept saying. "*This* amazing thing happened, and *that* miracle took place."

All the while I was thinking, *Please! Don't tell me another word.* You see, at the time we were between houses, living with our four kids in someone else's basement. I was homeschooling a first grader and getting up in the night with our youngest, besides keeping up with the two in between.

Every ounce of energy and focus was going to the kids. I was so hungry to be with God, but I didn't have time to go off to a weekend retreat. Jim was so elated, and all I could do was listen and feel miserable.

When Jim finally left the room, I leaned my head against the wall and silently cried, my tears releasing to God the depth of my hunger. I felt desperate because it seemed that I could do nothing to find a spare minute to be alone with Him.

Just then the Lord came to me in my desperation, and in that still, small voice inside He said, "Michal Ann, I'm God of the impossible. What's impossible for you is not impossible for Me. I'm going to start coming and visiting you in the night season."

I wasn't even sure I understood what He meant. But the most amazing thing began to happen. Night after night I began to dream. One night I dreamed a dear, sweet old gentleman came to me. I knew who He was at once. He was so kind and loving, and He loved the fragrance of my hair. He wanted me to simply lean near and hug Him so He could smell its fragrance. I'd never noticed that my hair had any kind of scent, but He did. He knew everything about me. In this way, night after night, God came wooing. We went on long walks down country lanes, and He told me about the preciousness of my life and revealed how cherished I am. I was given a gift of seeing myself through His loving eyes!

Yes, I believe that perhaps these dreams were, in a way, unusual. But in no way do I think I am unique or specially favored by God more than anyone else. He had a specific way of revealing His love to me at that time, and He has a very special, most wonderful way to reveal Himself to you too.

I'm telling you about my experience so that you will know one thing for sure: with God, nothing is impossible. Even though you may feel like your schedule is too full or too busy, and you don't know how you can squeeze out an additional moment, God Himself can make a way. In fact, He is already seeking out the times and places where He can meet alone with you. He's looking for the tiniest opening in your day or your night when He can make His wonderful presence known in a unique way in your life.

Reflect & Pray

1. How frantic is your pace of life? What steps can you take to pause and think of Him?

2. What is the best way you have found to enter the secret place with God and know His real presence with you every day? What can you adjust or cut out of your schedule so that you can add some quality God-time?

3. List a few things that seem impossible for you to accomplish. Now write a statement of faith that declares you will meet your goals with God's help.

4. God is yearning to commune with you. Pause now and listen to His voice calling you to Him even in the midst of your busy daily schedule.

Dear Lord of Creation, may I learn to hear your voice no matter my circumstances. Thank you for wanting to talk and walk with me throughout my day. In Jesus' name, amen.

Meeting God

> With all prayer and petition pray [with specific requests]
> at all times [on every occasion and in every season] in the
> Spirit, and with this in view, stay alert with all perseverance
> and petition [interceding in prayer] for all God's people.
>
> EPHESIANS 6:18

*Y*es, the dream gave me assurance of God's love and presence. No, the dream did not last. It was a catalyst, an invitation. It spurred me on to seek God because suddenly I knew that intimacy with Him was absolutely possible no matter where I was and no matter what kind of stress I was experiencing. I wish staying in that wonderful secret place with Him happened automatically, but it did not. Since then I've learned that we have to take practical steps to meet with the God who so obviously longs to meet with us.

How do we begin?

First, most of us have to disregard the idea that we have to be "specially called" to times of prayer. When we read 1 Thessalonians 5:17 where Paul tells us to "pray without ceasing" (KJV), we might think that prayer is meant only for "super saints." Maybe some people are gifted in a way in which they can repeat their prayer lists all the time. Or maybe we've grown up with a distorted view of what prayer really is! Maybe we're trying to approach prayer as a form of mental exercise—something that in our own natural power we can do.

The fact is that God calls every one of us to prayer. The thing we must realize, however, is this: *Before God calls us to prayer, He calls us to Himself.* When God says, "Come away, My beloved," He is calling every one of us (see Song of Solomon 8:14). *He is calling you.*

Second, we need to find a place to be entirely alone. Susanna Wesley literally had no place to go inside her own home to get away from her many children in order to be alone with the Lord. When she pulled her apron up over her head, her children knew it was time to leave her alone. Most of us have better living circumstances than Susanna Wesley. If you have a bathroom or even a large closet, you can find a place to be alone.

Third, we must also learn what it takes to quiet our own spirit. Because we're so bombarded by outside noise and information, we don't even know what we ourselves are like on the inside, and we can get totally out of touch with our own feelings and motives. We must begin to be quiet by disconnecting from the newspaper, the television, the Internet, the radio, and gab sessions with friends. We can then take time to search our hearts with the help of the Holy Spirit to find out what's really going on inside of us. Sometimes we don't even want to know what's going on "in there." But if we want to find the secret place with God, we must enter with our true selves. Keeping up false fronts and masks will hinder us from experiencing God's presence. As David says in his great psalm of confession, only truth and honesty in the inward parts will allow us to enter where God abides (see Psalm 51:6).

Fourth, we need help to prevent our minds from wandering. If you've ever tried to spend time alone with the Lord, you know what I mean. You seek quiet and a break, but the minute you sit down "the list" takes over your mind. You think, *I can't just sit here. There's wet laundry in the dryer, and I've got to pay this bill, and … and … and …* You realize you're not getting anywhere spiritually and you give up.

For this reason, *I recommend you enter into the secret place with God by meditating on His Word.* I can think of no better way to corral and direct your straying thoughts than to guide them along the spiritual pathways of truth laid out by God's Spirit. And of course, it is also important that we meditate on God's Word, because through His Word God builds up our faith by revealing Himself to us. There, in His Word, we see Him at work; we learn about His nature and character. We see Him act; we sense Him loving and winning back the world, and us, to Himself.

In each of these steps, we turn our hearts toward God. Each one makes possible the *fifth* thing we can do to prepare ourselves to meet with Him in the secret place; we must open ourselves to receive His love.

The strongest need we possess is our need to be loved. Most arguments we have with each other have to do with the issue of being loved. We each have inside us this huge vacuum that no human being can ever fill. Only God can fill the void we have within.

Praying only from our heads with our understanding doesn't accomplish anything because prayer is nothing more and nothing less than turning our heart fully toward God, opening up all of what we are to Him, and in turn receiving His love in place of our emptiness.

Opening to God and yielding is so difficult for many of us. What is it like to yield to Him? Consider Adam, just after he was created. There he was, a fine physical specimen made by God, perfect in every way. Yet there was no life in him. As Adam lay there on the ground, God bent down and was the One who breathed life into Adam. God is still doing that today, stooping to breathe life into our empty, needy souls. What did Adam do to receive this life? Nothing. He just lay there and let God do the breathing. In the same way, we must open ourselves to God, yield to Him, and simply allow Him to fill us.

Although I say "simply" allow God to fill you, it is a difficult instruction for us to grasp. We have such a works mentality built into us. We mentally carry around lists of the many things we must do to become worthy. Unfortunately, the Christian church can add to this pressure, making us feel that we need to do more to please God so that He will be "happy" with us. In actuality, all that we are required to do is relax and breathe; just breathe in the breath, the very Spirit of God who is always present with us.

And not only is He present with us, but there's also something even better. This is an incredible fact—the kingdom of God is within us, making God Himself accessible to us at any time.

Many truly great women of faith down through the ages have understood how to enter into that secret place with God. It's in the secret place of prayer that we find inspiration for the dull and dry times and comfort for the lonely and hurting times. Such mighty, truly noble Christian women knew how to exhale the concerns that sought to bind them as well as the misconceptions about God that might have kept them from approaching Him. They understood what it meant to empty themselves of all worldly preoccupations that can fill up the inner rooms of our souls and push Him out. They knew what it meant to inhale the peace that only comes from Him, like a spiritual fragrance, and then to pray, "Father, I want to meet with you in the secret place."

Reflect & Pray

1. Of the five steps that you can take to meet God in the secret place of prayer, which one most helped you see prayer in a more practical way? Why?

2. When disconnecting from distractions, which one is the hardest to ignore? How can you best manage this issue?

3. In what areas have you yielded your total self to God? What areas do you feel God is calling you to surrender more completely?

4. What does it mean for you to "inhale the peace that only comes from Him, like a spiritual fragrance"?

Dear heavenly Father, I want to meet you in the secret place where I know you are waiting for me with open arms. Please provide me the opportunity to exhale the concerns that bind me as well as any misconceptions about you that might keep me from approaching you. I pray that you will allow me to breathe in the breath, the very Spirit of God who is always present with me. In Jesus' name, amen.

Day 17

Enter the Secret Place

Now may the God of peace Himself sanctify you through and through [that is, separate you from profane and vulgar things, make you pure and whole and undamaged—consecrated to Him—set apart for His purpose]; and may your spirit and soul and body be kept complete and [be found] blameless at the coming of our Lord Jesus Christ.

1 THESSALONIANS 5:23

*H*ave you learned what it's like to have God's very presence fill you the way breath fills your lungs? You can easily enter into the secret place of your soul where God's Spirit dwells if you know the way.

The kind of prayer I am referring to is not about getting it right or about achieving a goal—the motivation for many of our prayers— neither is it about making yourself presentable to God before you ask to meet with Him. There is a kind of intimate praying that can only come about as we learn to strip away pretense and come, just as we are, into the inner chamber with our Lord and King.

Some of us look at other Christian women, especially "prayer warriors" or "great women of faith" and think, *If only I knew how to pray the way **she** prays.* Unfortunately, we engage in a kind of worldly thinking when it comes to prayer. We treat prayer as if we're going into another woman's home to see her decorating scheme and lovely fabrics, furniture selection, and colors. We think, *If only I could deck myself out like her. If only I could come before God the way she does—then my life with God would take off and my prayers would become powerful.*

Prayer that brings us into intimate experiences with God does not involve imitating another or reproducing their prayers. You are your own person; you are unique. And there is a place of intimacy with you that God cannot find with anyone else. He wants you to have a relationship with Him that no one else can enjoy. *And so God wants you to be just exactly who you are.*

One of the greatest spiritual problems many of us have is wishing we were someone else. We want to enjoy God's presence, but we think, *God, you really don't want to meet with me, do you?* Sister in Christ, God wants you to know that you can take yourself as you find yourself and start from there. You can't change your history; you can't change mistakes or undo wrong things from your past. *You can't remake yourself into somebody you're not.* So begin with the person you are today. Beginning with God is like standing in front of a sign in the mall that says, "You are here." God wants you to say, "God, I'm here! Just as I am, I come."

Being able to enter into the deep love and peace of God in prayer is not about getting rid of flaws and faults. If it were we would spend all our time trying to make ourselves perfect, and that never works. Instead, it's being in the presence of someone—the wonderful God who has said, "I am with you always" (Matthew 28:20 NIV). Entering your secret place requires nothing more than coming, for He says, "Everything and everyone that the Father has given Me will come to Me, and I won't turn any of them away" (John 6:37 CEV).

The only requirement for finding our way to the secret place with God is just to begin. We begin by abandoning ourselves to God, which means seeking Him and learning to rest in His divine presence no matter what our circumstances.

If we abandon ourselves to God, we train our souls to rest in Him. We trust that He is in control of our lives, not only when everything goes well, but also when everything goes wrong. We trust that He has not abandoned us, and that He knows what's best for us by allowing different situations and circumstances into our lives. We make a deliberate choice to believe that He is working something bigger into us than what we can accomplish ourselves. I am not saying this is easy. It's not. But by abandoning ourselves to God and totally laying down our lives, we leave all our cares and concerns in His loving hands.

If we want the peace of God that only He can give, we must abandon ourselves completely to Him. Abandonment is the key that unlocks our entry to the secret place where our King and heavenly Bridegroom dwells.

Abandonment is the means God uses to reveal His mysteries to us. There are so many mysteries about God which He longs to reveal to us, His Bride. One of the greatest mysteries is the way God transforms us from who we are now into women who bear the marks of Jesus Christ. Paul referred to this mystery when he said, "I bear on my body the marks of Jesus" (Galatians 6:17 NIV). If we love and abandon ourselves to God, as Paul did, we will be transformed into His image.

I believe that Paul was describing the "narrow way," a way that stands open before each one of us (see Matthew 7:13–14). To find your way to this place in God requires giving Him the keys to everything: children, husbands, families, homes, possessions, friends, jobs, and our dreams. We must place everything into His hands and leave it there for Him to do with as He sees fit.

What will it take to produce this kind of abandonment in us? It does not come easily and it takes great faith. The greater our faith, the more we know God, and the better we know Him, the easier it will be to abandon ourselves freely without the slightest hesitation or holding back.

When we become completely united with Him spirit, soul, and body, the barriers of doubt, fear, and pride will all melt in the warmth of His love (see 1 Thessalonians 5:23). We will come into a place where peace, love, and eternal strength are ours because we are one with Him, peacefully resting in the wonder of that love. Throughout history, great men and women alike have found their way into the secret place where God dwells. They have entered that place by learning the secrets of quiet prayer and how to abandon themselves completely to God. They knew how to become His Bride and were consumed with the love and presence of God as they yielded themselves completely and became one with Him.

Reflect & Pray

1. Have you wished to be like someone else? Knowing that God created you as a unique individual, how do you think He feels when you want to imitate someone else?

2. Write a short prayer thanking God for exactly what and who you are.

3. "If we want the peace of God that only He can give, we must abandon ourselves completely to Him." In what area do you want to abandon yourself completely to God?

4. Reflect how God's peace, love, and eternal strength are ours because we are one with Him. Peacefully rest in the wonder of His love.

Dear Father of peace and love, lead me out of the storms and stresses of life that distract me and keep me from knowing you. More than anything else, I want to know you. I want to open wide my heart and life to you. Guide me by your Holy Spirit to the secret place where you can reveal yourself in wonder, majesty, and holiness in me and through me to a lost world. In Jesus' name, amen.

Day 18

Intimacy with God

"For the LORD your God is a consuming fire;
He is a jealous (impassioned) God [demanding what
is rightfully and uniquely His]."

DEUTERONOMY 4:24

*I*ntimacy with God—hmm, sounds romantic doesn't it? But our God is holy and His holiness is a consuming fire (see Deuteronomy 4:24). How does God draw us closer to Himself? He does so by kindling a love in our hearts for Him and a deep desire to be close to Him. We become like moths that are drawn out of the darkness toward a great light—drawn by a force from beyond ourselves.

As we get closer, something else begins to happen. The fire of God begins to make us uncomfortable. The light of His holiness begins to scorch the dross and the chaff within us. We experience turmoil as we become painfully aware of our sins, shortcomings, and unworthiness to be in His beautiful, holy presence. We also become aware that we have been drawn to idolatry—false passions of the soul and flesh that have kept us trapped in worldliness.

That turmoil grows deeper and stronger until it wages a battle over our very soul. We long for Him and sense the seal of the Holy Spirit, like the engagement ring pledged as a promise of a coming wedding day (see Ephesians 4:30). Yet all of our failings, anger, jealousy, and lust are revealed before our eyes. In torment we cry out, believing that He could not possibly love or want us as we are.

If only we could understand! Our heavenly Lover already sees and knows everything about us. And although He is aware of all our faults, He nevertheless calls us to Himself. Unfortunately, our awareness of our sin and our sense of unworthiness cause us to resist Him, holding us back from running into His arms and abandoning ourselves to Him. But there in His wonderful, gracious embrace He longs to cover all our weaknesses, needs, and sickness of soul.

We quickly discover that there is only one thing to do. In the moment of our greatest soul-agony, when we feel ourselves to be the most useless and unworthy in His eyes, we must run to Him and cry out: "Help me, my Lord and my God!"

As we rush toward Him, the wind of desperate desire fuels the flame of His passion, burning away our dross and chaff with consuming love. In this moment we begin to understand why He has allowed all the mistakes, sins, failures, and disappointments. Frances Thompson's famous poem, "The Hound of Heaven," echoes the voice of God, revealing a great mystery of His wonderful ways:

> All which I took from thee I did but take,
> Not for thy harms,
> But that thou might'st seek it in My arms.
> All which thy child's mistake
> Fancies as lost, I have stored for thee at home:
> Rise, clasp My hand, and come![1]

We long to experience the fire of our Lover, but we're afraid to run into His arms, knowing He is a "living flame of love," as John of the Cross called Him so well.[2] We are afraid of the process it takes to fully embrace Him and be caught up in Him forever.

So we hang on to worldly things—passions, interests, positions, power, possessions, people—all in an attempt to anchor ourselves here on earth and to keep from running to Him. We worry: *What will He ask of me? What will He force me to give up?* We attempt to bargain our way out of our perceived losses. *What will He let me keep?* We are blanketed with condemnation because we know we should not consider earthly "treasures" to be more valuable than Him. But we do.

Instead of being consumed by Him in the blissful joy of godly passion and the ecstasy of spiritual freedom, we are consumed by guilt instead. We know we should want Him only, but because we hold back we begin to believe that we don't qualify for His love. Hopelessness begins to pull us down into discouragement and depression.

We look up in the midst of our turmoil to see a man standing before us. As we look at Him—Jesus, the living, loving Son of God and God Himself in the flesh—He captures us with the intense look of love in His eyes. His heart calls us so tenderly: "Just let go of your struggle. This minute. Let it go … and come to Me!"

We begin to walk toward Him, staring into His eyes of love, and we let go of all our fear and resistance. Now, we begin to run. In our rush, the Holy Spirit breathes upon the embers of our smoldering passion, setting our hearts ablaze with love for Him.

At last, we become the Fire Bride of God.

Where she once feared the fire, to her own delighted amazement she now cries out for more. "More fire!" The intensity of heat has tried her heart and it is becoming transformed into precious, purified gold. Her heart is pure because it is finding completion in Him and in nothing more.

Her heart will never again be polluted by other, lesser loves. For her heart is no longer hers—she has given it to Him. Her will is no longer hers, for she longs to lose it in abandonment to His. Her life and His are one.

Reflect & Pray

1. Have you ever felt scorched by God's refining fire? What does God's refreshing grace feel like after being refined?

2. We all experience turmoil as we become aware of our sins and shortcomings. During the turmoil, how hard is it to remember that God's love and mercy are more powerful than any sin you commit?

3. Write what it means to you to be the Fire Bride of God.

4. What apprehensions do you have when you think about going through His refining fire? Read the following Scriptures: Job 23:10; Psalm 12:6; Zechariah 13:9; and Revelation 3:18. How do they change your perspective about being His Fire Bride?

Father God, thank you that your salvation is full and complete for both now and eternity. Through the wisdom of those who have walked this way before, and through your Holy Spirit present deep within, heal my wounds. Fill the empty longings deep inside my soul that gape like open cuts driving me to seek comfort and satisfaction in everything but you. Open my eyes, Lord, as you opened the eyes of great women of the faith who have gone before. Let me see you and you alone. In Jesus' name, amen.

Spiritual Intimacy:
Madame Jeanne Guyon (1648–1717)

> Now having been asked by the Pharisees when the kingdom
> of God would come, He replied, "The kingdom of God is not
> coming with signs to be observed or with a visible display;
> nor will people say, 'Look! Here it is!' or, 'There it is!' For the
> kingdom of God is among you [because of My presence]."
>
> LUKE 17:20–21

The wisdom I have gained from Madame Guyon's life and writings has helped me to understand why difficult things have happened in my life and in the lives of my children. I've been able to pass onto them godly wisdom that is guiding them in their lives through troublesome and uncertain circumstances. Consequently, I see myself growing deeper in the knowledge of God, and I see myself becoming the godly mother I have longed to be. I don't know about you, but to me that kind of spiritual growth is more precious than gold!

Amazingly, it was never Madame Guyon's intent to write a book of any kind. As it happened, in the Catholic faith there are men and women known as spiritual directors—people who are responsible for the spiritual growth of anyone who was serious about faith and wanted to come under their guidance. Jeanne would go to her spiritual directors and pose all her questions. Depending upon whom she was receiving direction from at a particular time, she might or might not receive spiritual help and clarity. The main reason we have her writings at all is because her spiritual directors commanded her to write about her spiritual experiences and insights as a matter of obedience. Ironically, her questions and beliefs raised suspicion in the Church and she was put in jail as a possible heretic.

Madame Guyon's profound insight came to us from a cold, dirty, stone prison cell where she wrote in defense of the one belief upon which her faith rested—that entering in unity with God happens only as we abandon ourselves totally to Him.

She said, "… you [must become] fully convinced that it is on the nothing in man that God establishes His greatest works … He destroys that He might build. For when He is about to rear His sacred temple in us, He first totally razes that vain and pompous edifice that human art and power had erected. And from its horrible ruins, a new structure is formed, by His power only."[1]

In this one piece of writing, we see the heart of Madame Guyon. Revealed is the essence of a faith that was rich, strong, alive, and unbeatable, no matter what rose up against her. So how did she find her way into the secret place with God, the place where we long to go?

By reading spiritual works, such as the writings of St. Frances DeSales, Jeanne's soul deepened. Eventually she began to spend more time with her prayer book; she was still trying to connect with that distant, elusive voice that seemed to call and then fade. The streets were full of beggars, destitute widows, and orphans, and Jeanne gave all she had to the poor. Gathering a small group of poor people together, she taught the catechism.

It was at this time that Jeanne discovered the writings of a woman known as Madame de Chantel. Never before had she heard anyone speak of the things this woman of faith talked about, especially what she called "mental prayer"—what we know as praying to God freely from the heart. According to Madame de Chantel, it was the beginning of the way into the secret place of union with God.

More time would pass before Jeanne made the discovery that

turned all her sufferings into spiritual gold. Jeanne married a man who mistreated her, and shortly after the birth of her second child she met a man from the Order of St. Francis. He had lived in solitude for five years, caught up in the love of God, and had just emerged from this long retreat with a kind of glow about him that was unearthly. Jeanne's father, knowing her devotion to God, arranged for her to meet with him.

Suddenly, nothing was easier for her than prayer. Hours flew by like moments, and the joy and intensity of her devotion increased! As she put it, "The fervency of my love allowed me no intermission."[2]

Now she was able to bear the ill treatment of her husband and mother-in-law, no matter how insulting or rigorous, silently and without turmoil. She was swept away from the cares of the world around her, having found that place inside where she could go and meet with God. Within her own soul at all times she could retreat to a secret and holy place where she could spend time with Him.

In time, Jeanne became so attuned to God's presence that she scarcely knew what she was eating. Occasionally she missed what people were saying to her, and she went for long periods without speaking. A Barnabite Friar, Francois LaCombe, not only believed in Jeanne's spiritual wisdom but encouraged her to write a small book, which was published in 1685 under the title *A Short and Easy Method of Prayer*.

We have much to learn from her. First, many of us today are looking for spiritual experiences. We run here and there, to one revival after another, seeking spiritual gifts and anointing. But very early in her walk with the Lord, Jeanne Guyon realized that "spiritual experience" can get in the way of and delay the work of the

Holy Spirit in us, which is destined to bring us into what she called "true union" with Him.

Writing about our need to seek nothing other than union with God, she said, "[The prayer that brings union with God] … is far above … transports or visions, for visions are in the inferior powers of the soul and cannot produce true union. The soul must not dwell or rely upon them or be impeded by them. They are but favors and gifts, the Giver alone must be our object and aim."[3]

She warns us against loving visions, stressing how we can overemphasize them and be deceived by them. Visions are apt to create pride and vanity in the soul. Instead of attending to, loving, extolling, and praising God, we can dwell on our gifts and visions which can lead us astray.

Second, she also warns against overemphasizing "spiritual feelings" or "ecstasies." She wrote, "Ecstasies arise from a perceptible delight. They may be termed a kind of spiritual sensuality, wherein the soul, by letting it go too far by reason of the sweetness it finds in them, falls imperceptibly into decay."[4]

Many of her most brilliant insights come to us out of her times of loss and desperate weakness. She learned to press into God as a young woman with everything against her. Later in life when she was ill and could no longer visit the poor she loved so dearly, she would still insist that it was for love that God allowed even that which is most dear to your soul—your calling, gifting, or anointing—to fall away so that you might be drawn closer to Him alone.

Most importantly of all, Madame Guyon's life teaches us this wonderful truth about how we can experience intimacy with God. For she wrote: "It is Jesus Christ Himself, the real and essential Word, who is in the center of the soul that is disposed for receiving Him. Never one moment ceases from His living, fruitful, and divine operation."[5]

Reflect & Pray

1. Have you ever been inspired to write about your experiences with God? If yes, have you shared your writings with others? If no, what other venues can you think of to share your relationship with God?

2. Which Christian book (or books) has been the most inspiring and enlightening? What makes it your favorite?

3. Madame Guyon went to jail as a possible heretic. If there were such a thing in this country as "anti-Christian police," what evidence would they have against you to put you in jail?

4. "Ecstasies arise from a perceptible delight. They may be termed a kind of spiritual sensuality, wherein the soul, by letting it go too far by reason of the sweetness it finds in them, falls imperceptibly into decay." Write about what this means to you.

Dear heavenly Father, thank you for women who were so empowered by your Word and the words of other saints that they stood strong for you and daily sought to drink in your goodness. May I be so moved. In Jesus' name, amen.

The Secret Place
of Teresa of Avila (1515–1582)

"For this reason I am telling you,
whatever things you ask for in prayer [in accordance with
God's will], believe [with confident trust] that you have
received them, and they will be given to you."

MARK 11:24

*A*t an early age, while other children ran and played, Teresa sought for ways to be alone with her Lord. She prayed often and turned her bedroom at home into a sanctuary where she hung a picture of Christ speaking with the Samaritan woman at the well. Teresa pleaded over and over again in prayer, "Lord, give me of that water that I may not thirst."[1]

One day, something shocking happened that put an end to everything worldly in Teresa's life. She fell to the floor as if dead. Many believed that she lapsed into a coma, although little proof has been offered. Doctors found no pulse, and all attempts to revive her failed.

Thinking she was dead, the doctors left and a priest anointed her body with holy oils; prayers for the dead were recited and nuns set the body aside to stiffen before burial. Her family made funeral preparations and a grave was prepared.

Four days later, her father and her brother witnessed a supernatural fire as it hit her body. Her eyelids began blinking, her arms moved, blood rushed to her face, and she rose inexplicably. While all had been judging Teresa as dead, she was having a heavenly vision, seeing her family and communities of nuns.

Then, some time later, another dramatic event took place. Teresa had a spiritual encounter with God so intense that she eventually questioned her own sanity. She saw the risen Jesus, not through physical eyes, but as in a vision through her heart.

When she was questioned by the nuns regarding her experience, at the point of tears, she replied, "Because He told me so, over and over again."[2]

Though she had walked through the dark night of the soul with great physical pain and affliction, from this time on it seemed as though the tangible presence of Jesus was with her. She was now ruined for heaven's sake, no longer to converse with men but with the angels.

Still another even more intense encounter awaited Teresa of Avila some years later. In her autobiography, *The Life of Teresa of Jesus,* Teresa wrote of a shining angel plunging a flaming, golden arrow into her heart: "When he drew it out I thought he was carrying off with him the deepest part of me; and he left me all on fire with a great love of God."[3] She described the angel as small and very beautiful. Reflecting upon this encounter, she considered that this angel from the Lord was so illuminated that he had to be one of the very highest of the angels: the cherubim. He thrust the fiery dart into her heart several times, piercing her down to her innermost organs, leaving her with an intense love for God. She became possessed by God's love.[4]

Teresa used these descriptive terms to paint a vivid picture of the stages of cultivating a life of prayer. The beginner in prayer toils, fetching water from the well. The effort is entirely his, as he attempts to fill the bucket with water and replenish the flowers of the garden. If he persists, his love for the flowers will exceed the strain of work. The privilege of seeing the arid land blossom will produce humility and endurance that will cause his soul to richly prosper.

In the second stage, the gardener uses a waterwheel and buckets. He can draw more water for the garden than before with much less effort if the long hours required do not become wearisome. This second stage can be a time of trial when weeding and pruning is being done to the soul. Here the believer learns the *Prayer of Quiet* and the beginning of pure contemplation.

The third stage of prayer is when the Lord is more active, providing water by a spring or stream running through the garden. There is now no question of turning back; the delight is too sweet, it is a glorious folly, a heavenly madness in which true wisdom is acquired. Teresa said this was when Mary and Martha, action and contemplation, are in perfect harmony, though not yet entirely absorbed into God. The soul is free from worries and becomes content. God is now the gardener and the supply of water is abundant.

The last stage of the call to the secret place is where the garden is watered by rain and the gardener has nothing to do but to watch the flowers grow. This is what Madame Jeanne Guyon and many others called the *Prayer of Union*. The rain brings this union about from heaven itself. After this type of prayer, Teresa found herself in a state of overwhelming tenderness, bathed in tears of joy. Here you know God.

Love was what it was all about to Teresa; her life of prayer was the story of an intimate friendship with God. Teresa of Avila and others who have known the secret place have cherished the inner courts of the Lord. They simply followed in the paths of other forerunners who had gone before them. But remember Mary and Martha are to be wedded together. The authentic inward journey should lead to empowered outward works.

We each leave a shadow in this life that will fall upon others. That is what happens when people walk in the light of God's love—the shadow of His presence is cast upon others from our lives.

And so Teresa's legacy was that the secret place became her dwelling place. All this happened despite poor health that only became increasingly fragile as she grew older.

An acting Provincial called Antonio of Jesus sent her on an unexpected journey. He was jealous, cold, and insensitive to Teresa's ill health and physical needs. She humbly obeyed his orders, contrary to the advice of friends. In October 1582, after finally reaching Alba de Tormes, the ailing Teresa of Jesus died from exhaustion and near starvation.

Perhaps the best way to sum up the life of Teresa is in her own words written toward the end of her life. Listen to her through them, for they describe this mystical poet's great trust:

> Let nothing trouble you,
> Let nothing scare you,
> All is fleeing,
> God alone is unchanging,
> Patience,
> Everything obtains.
> Who possesses God
> Nothing wants.
> God alone suffices.[5]

Reflect & Pray

1. What do you think happened to Teresa that made her seem dead for four days? Have you witnessed or heard of a similar experience?

2. According to Teresa of Avila, there are four ways to cultivate a life of prayer. Write each in your own words.

3. Teresa was empowered when her heart was pierced by a flaming, golden arrow. In what way would an experience like this affect you?

4. Write a short poem that expresses your love for God.

Dear Father God, I pray that you will empower me to be as accepting of your communication with me as Teresa of Avila was. May I not be afraid of the gifts you may want to share with me. May I gracefully and thankfully accept all that you have for me to fulfill my God-given destiny. In Jesus' name, amen.

Powerful Songs:
Fanny Crosby (1820–1915)

Now faith is the assurance (title deed, confirmation) of things
hoped for (divinely guaranteed), and the evidence of things
not seen [the conviction of their reality—faith comprehends
as fact what cannot be experienced by the physical senses].

HEBREWS 11:1

In her time, Fanny Crosby was considered of equal stature with colleagues Dwight L. Moody and Ira Sankey. She was renowned as a preacher and lecturer and spent much of her life involved in home missions. People would line up for blocks to hear her speak.

She didn't start writing until she was in her forties; nevertheless, she wrote about 9,000 hymns. Her style was revolutionary for her day. Rather than following the standard, traditional form, she expressed thoughts and prayers in common words that touched the heart of worship in believers. The passion of her love for God drew the lost into the kingdom of God.

Fanny also composed more than 1,000 poems and played the harp and organ in concert. So many accomplishments seem incredible for any one person, but all the more when you realize that these talents were beautifully expressed through a woman who was blind from infancy!

Fanny (Frances Jane) Crosby was born into a family that was fiercely proud of their history and heritage. This rural family's heritage could be traced back to William Brewster, who sailed on the Mayflower in 1620 and was a founding father of Plymouth Plantation.

Grandmother Eunice took a great interest in her granddaughter who had become blind shortly after her birth, and the two became very close during the first five years of Fanny's life. With the passage of time, it became painfully apparent that Fanny would not regain her sight, and so Eunice became determined to give Fanny every advantage in training. She could not bear to see Fanny go through life treated as if she were helpless and having to be utterly dependent on others.

Eunice was a "firm believer in prayer" and understood it was the key to a successful Christian life. She considered prayer a "close communication with her loving Savior."[1] Everything she believed about God and the importance and place of prayer was freely poured into Fanny. Grandmother Eunice spent her days teaching little Fanny how to live life by calling on God for every need and believing in His goodness and His certain authority and power to accomplish every good work and care for every need.

Fanny learned to trust Jesus Christ and to rest and rejoice in Him. This wise classroom of her grandmother's imparted to Fanny a place of faith and an ability to bear her sufferings and difficulties with great grace and joy, knowing that God was always walking with her, leading, guiding, and loving her.

Thus began Fanny Crosby's education. She sat with her family in the evenings and listened as the family read by the fireplace such works as *The Iliad, The Odyssey, Paradise Lost, The Tales of Robin Hood,* and the Bible. Eunice became her granddaughter's eyes, describing her surroundings to her in careful detail. Because Fanny could at times distinguish certain hues, Eunice was able to bring definition to colors.

In the year 1848, cholera broke out and Fanny contracted the disease. She recovered, but her close brush with death made her think about dying. Would she be ready to meet God? She had believed in God and His goodness but had never experienced conversion. During this time of seeking and soul-searching, Fanny dreamed she visited a dying man. The man asked her if she would meet him in heaven after their deaths. She responded in the dream that by God's help, she would—the same response she had given her grandmother. The dream ended as the man said, "Remember, you promised a dying man!"

The experience drew Fanny to a deeper place of seeking God. She attended revival meetings and went to the altar twice, feeling nothing had changed. However, the third time she went to the altar, something happened:

> During the fifth verse of "Alas, and Did My Savior Bleed?" Fanny prayed: "Here Lord, I give myself away. 'Tis all that I can do." Suddenly Fanny felt "my very soul was flooded with celestial light." She jumped to her feet, shouting, "Hallelujah! Hallelujah!" She said, "For the first time I realized that I had been trying to hold the world in one hand and the Lord in the other."[2]

Fanny's life was dramatically changed. She called it her "November experience." From that point on, her life was totally dedicated to God. A desire to do His will alone consumed her, and all other desires fell away into the dust. It is from this experience that many of her later hymns were birthed.

Fanny associated with the poor in spirit, slum dwellers, alcoholics, and prisoners. She gave herself to a life of simplicity, giving away money and aid to those in need. She knew God's heart for the poor and needy, and in embracing them she embraced Him. One of the keys to the secret place is having a tender place in our hearts for the alien, the orphan, and the widow.

Fanny knew the power of distraction and would purpose to have time alone with God in the long night watches. She daily carved a place to be alone with Him, even though it meant sleepless nights. He was her rest and peace.

By employing all her energies to realize the full maturity and effectiveness of her gifting, Fanny learned how to apply herself. She harnessed the strength of her mind to the Spirit of God, enabling her mind to become an effectual tool. She brought her mind—her mental ability—into the secret place.

In addition, Fanny learned to embrace concern and even criticism from others, allowing them to work true humility into her life. She established a lifestyle of selflessness, not giving room in her heart to pride. She learned to receive from God and others, whether in gentleness or in conflict, and ask God to make her heart right within her.

Reflect & Pray

1. Do you or someone you know have a disability? How has God brought good from that disability?
2. Many people would have been discouraged about being sightless. Who helped keep Fanny focused on things other than her blindness?
3. List the names of those who have helped you through life. Write a thank-you note to that person.
4. Read a favorite Fanny Crosby hymn and write a few verses. Think about her life as you consider the words she wrote.

Dear Father in heaven, thank you for the talents you give each of us. I pray that you will show me how to use the gifts you have given me to your glory. In Jesus' name, amen.

Day 22

Innovator and Educator:
Susanna Wesley (1669–1742)

Train up a child in the way he should go [teaching him to
seek God's wisdom and will for his abilities and talents],
Even when he is old he will not depart from it.

PROVERBS 22:6

More than 2,000 Puritan pastors were forced to stop prac-
ticing their faith under the reign of English Royalist King
Charles II. Nevertheless, Puritan pastor Dr. Samuel Annesley flatly
refused. The consequences of opposing the king of England were
harsh. Samuel was evicted from his clerical position, harassed, and
forced to undergo hardship at the hands of the authorities. Still,
he never wavered from his courageous convictions. Born into this
religiously tumultuous time was Samuel's impressionable young
daughter, Susanna.

Susanna married Church of England clergyman Samuel Wesley
when she was twenty years old and eventually had nineteen children, a number of whom died at young ages. When her husband
went to London for a period of time, Susanna began earnestly meeting with each of her children individually to determine the condition of their souls and their commitment to God. She searched for
the most impressive sermons she could find and read them to her
gathering of hungry hearts. Soon the attendance grew to standing
room only—about two hundred people!

When Susanna wrote a letter to her husband Samuel inform-
ing him about the meetings, Samuel responded expressing many

concerns. He was unsure they should continue. Susanna wrote back in a very straightforward manner, going head-to-head with each one of his arguments with clarity and humility. After receiving her response, Samuel gave his approval. The meetings continued, and both the family and community experienced the grace of God in a beautiful way.

Susanna's success, however, unleashed furious anger and jealousy from the curate, Mr. Inman. He wrote a letter to Samuel, accusing Susanna of holding illegal religious meetings. Afraid her gatherings would bring disapproval from the church and ruin his future ministerial career, Samuel changed his stance and asked Susanna to stop the meetings.

Susanna's reply to this latest challenge is worthy of quoting, at least in part. The following statements are taken from her letter to Samuel:

> I shall not inquire how it was possible that you should be prevailed on by the senseless clamors of two or three of the worst of your parish, to condemn what you so lately approved. ... It is plain in fact that this one thing has brought more people to church than ever anything did in so short a time. We used not to have above twenty to twenty-five at evening service, whereas we have now between two and three hundred; which are more than ever came before to hear Inman in the morning. ... Now, I beseech you, weigh all these things in an impartial balance: on the one side, the honor of almighty God, the doing much good to many souls, and the friendship of the best among whom we live; on the other, the senseless objections of a few scandalous persons ... and when you have duly considered all things, let me have your positive determination. ... If you do, after

all, think fit to dissolve this assembly, do not tell me that you desire me to do it, for that will not satisfy my conscience; but send me your positive command, in such full and express terms as may absolve me from all guilt and punishment, for neglecting this opportunity of doing good, when you and I shall appear before the great and awful tribunal of our Lord Jesus Christ.[1]

What fire was burning in her soul! There is no record of Samuel writing back and demanding that Susanna stop the meetings. They continued until he returned home.

Samuel reaped great benefit from his wife's efforts. His children were being spiritually nurtured. His parish was growing considerably in attendance and in the grace of God. His neighbors, who before had fired their guns off in front of his home terrorizing the children, and who probably had been responsible for setting their home on fire, were now supporting them for the first time. His children felt secure enough to now play freely outside. The most important benefit of all was that the form and structure of Susanna's meetings would eventually make up the basis for the entire Methodist movement.

All this was accomplished by a woman's commitment to nurturing in her children a love for God. God lit a fire in Susanna's soul that would eventually ignite many souls around the world. She discovered a balance in walking within the boundaries of understandings of her time period and yet daring to step out and do something for God's sake. She honored her husband and submitted herself to him, but she was confident enough to be different, to do what had never been done before in the midst of great criticism.

Susanna was an innovator in education. She believed in a good education, including religious training for both boys and girls equally, and she was convinced that the only way she could be sure it would happen was to do it herself. She actually developed extensive teaching manuals, including three theological manuals. The first discussed the order and design of creation and how it testified to God's existence. The second manual dealt with the great doctrines of the Christian faith using the Apostle's Creed. The third manual expounded upon the Ten Commandments, teaching the major tenets of divine moral law. She also wrote many theologically instructive letters to her children.

Susanna cared for nothing more on the earth than the salvation of her children's souls. Her writings were filled with understanding and instruction. She wrote concerning the sin of the will, the sin of the imagination, the sin of the memory, and the sin of the passions of the soul. She said that "sin is the greatest contradiction imaginable to His most holy nature."[2] About God, she wrote that He is "infinite purity, absolutely separated from all moral imperfection."[3] "He is goodness, and his most holy will cannot swerve or decline from what is so. He always wills what is absolutely best; nor can He possibly be deceived or deceive anyone."[4]

Through her children, especially John and Charles and their Methodist movement, Susanna touched the entire world. Her message of devotion to God and hunger to see lost souls come to God was much needed in the society of eighteenth-century England, where true religious conviction had become a rare commodity. Reason was exalted above the Bible, and Christianity was reduced to a code of ethics. Nearly lost was the understanding that sin must be forgiven and cleansed by a miracle-working God who had become man and died on a cross.

Reflect & Pray

1. God has called believers to spread the gospel to all corners of the world, and He invites us to start at home. How have you educated your children or other family members about the saving grace of God?

2. Although Susanna respected her husband, she disagreed with him about continuing to conduct the meetings. How do you disagree with your spouse or another person? Does that person respect your opinion? Why or why not?

3. Susanna wrote concerning the sin of the will and the sin of the imagination. Write a brief description of each in your own words.

4. She also wrote about "the sin of the memory, the sin of the passions of the soul." How do these apply to you?

Help me, O Lord, to make true use of all disappointments and calamities in this life, in such a way that they may unite my heart more closely with you. Cause them to separate my affections from worldly things and inspire my soul with more vigor in the pursuit of true happiness. Until this temper of mind be attained, I can never enjoy any settled peace, much less a calm serenity. You only, O God, can satisfy my immortal soul and bestow those spiritual pleasures that alone are proper to its nature. Grant me grace to stay and center my soul in you; to confine its desire, hopes, and expectations of happiness to you alone; and calmly to attend to the seasons of your providence and to have a firm, habitual resignation to your will. Enable me to love you, my God, with all my heart, with all my mind, and with all my strength. So to love you as to desire you. So to desire you as to be uneasy without you, without your favor and without some such resemblance to you as my nature in this imperfect state can bear. Amen.[5]

Day 23

The Sisterhood of Mary: Basilea Schlink (1904–2001)

> I can do all things [which He has called me to do] through
> Him who strengthens and empowers me [to fulfill His
> purpose—I am self-sufficient in Christ's sufficiency; I am
> ready for anything and equal to anything through Him who
> infuses me with inner strength and confident peace.]

PHILIPPIANS 4:13

While Basilea Schlink set out to discover the world as a young German woman, Hitler's influence was beginning to emerge. She began her studies in social welfare in 1923; at the same time, Hitler was attempting his first revolution, severely shaking the economy and creating inflation and the rationing of bread. As her nation was shaken to the core by political upheaval, Basilea's heart experienced its own kind of unrest. She was coming to grips with interior issues of true humility and repentance from sin, pride, and ambition.

She stated, "In my childhood and early youth it was always the same. When my sinful nature sought satisfaction, God sent me a cross so that a part of me had to die."[1]

Born in Darmstadt, Germany, on October 21, 1904, Basilea's heart from an early age was turned toward the Lord. Although she was high-spirited and enjoyed as many activities as other girls of her age, the call of God echoed deep in her soul. At the age of 20, Basilea's prayer was, "Preserve this inner life, but take away my self-esteem. All that I have comes from you and all the good in me can only be attributed to you, Lord Jesus. That I know very well."[2]

As a young woman, Basilea longed for someone to lead her to God. Finding no one, she worked hard to improve herself. Living without the transforming power of God soon brought her to the end of her striving. She realized she needed a revelation of God in her heart. In 1922, God answered her plea, and she beheld Jesus inwardly as the crucified Lord. She knew that she had come into the saving knowledge of Jesus Christ.

Revelation of the Father's love began to flow into her. The mystery of the grace of God unfolded in her heart and undid the works of the flesh. From this experience was birthed deep desire. Basilea longed to learn how to pray and grow in God's love. During these early days, Jesus Himself led her and taught her. She became aware that the former activities that brought her pleasure actually grieved the Holy Spirit, and so out of love for Him she let go of those things.

In 1930, Basilea attended the University in Berlin to work on her Ph.D. in psychology. She lived part of this time with her friend Erika, and she began to feel that God planned for the two of them to found and build up a ministry. During this time also, Basilea felt convicted to live a celibate life.

In 1933, at the height of Nazi National Socialism, Basilea's Jewish professors were forced to relinquish their positions. From 1933 to 1935, this young student held the position of national president of the Women's Division of the German Student Christian Movement. As part of the government-resisting Confessing Church, Basilea was used to influence the Christian student group to reject a paragraph stating that only German (Aryan) girls would be permitted to attend the meetings.

As Basilea traveled from place to place, she spoke on the power of Jesus' blood, His victory over the enemy, and His triumphant return. She covered Jesus' second coming, God's plan of salvation for Israel, the city of God, heaven and hell, the blessings of suffering, and how to overcome.

For years she prayed, "Grant me love, love which is not irritable or resentful, which bears all things, hopes all things, believes all things, endures all things."[3] God taught her the way of humility, to cease from self-justification, and to endure with patience and forbearance. His perfect love was to become her life's message.

On September 11, 1944, an air raid was leveled against Darmstadt. Buildings were toppled everywhere. Yet this black cloud contained a silver lining. It so sobered the girls with whom Erika and Basilea had been working that the change in their lives unleashed revival in their area.

These young women were seized with the intense need for personal repentance. As they spent more time in prayer, the Lord dealt with Erika and Basilea concerning the sins of their nation. During the war years, they had spent time in prayer over personal issues, but had they cried out for national sins? Had they repented for the prisoners of war and for the millions of Jews who were slaughtered? They had thought they were devoting their lives to God, but had they seen their lives in light of the sin of their nation? Great conviction fell upon them. Revival came from the ashes of Darmstadt.

Now the stage was being set for the foundation of a dream held within Basilea's heart. It would be called the Evangelical Sisterhood of Mary. It would grow to be an ecumenical community of women living in an attitude of contrition and fellowship in bridal love for Jesus. They would stand in the gap for their nation. Identifying Germany's sins as their own, the Sisters of Mary would cry out for mercy and forgiveness.

Basilea Schlink accomplished many things during her lifetime, much more than can be recounted here. Throughout her life, her primary goal was to love Jesus and to call others to love Him as our wonderful Bridegroom should be loved. Her many written works resulted from this devotion in her heart for Him. The effects of her love and devotion continue to bless those in many nations.

Basilea went to be with the Lord on March 21, 2001, but her work and vision for the Sisterhood of Mary continues. This community is dedicated to Christian radio ministry and to Christian literature. The Sisterhood publishes tracts in ninety languages which are distributed on five continents. Radio and television programs are broadcast in twenty-three languages. But more important than the programs and all the efforts is the fire of His love and the call to the secret place.

Reflect & Pray

1. Do you have a true spiritual friend? If yes, what do you appreciate about that person? If not, what do you think a true spiritual friend would be like?

2. Although you probably have not experienced an air raid, has there been a life-altering circumstance or situation in your life that made you change direction? What happened?

3. In what ways can you identify with how Basilea was praying for personal matters when she could have been praying for a nation that was causing great harm?

4. Describe the kind of legacy you want to leave behind. What steps can you take today to make that legacy one your family and friends will remember and appreciate?

Dear God of redemption, thank you for the many chances you give me to redeem myself. Thank you for accepting my flaws and miscommunications. I ask you to show me the "big picture" so I pray effectively and purposefully. In Jesus' name, amen.

End-Time Handmaidens: Gwen Shaw (1924-2013)

"Before I formed you in the womb I knew you
[and approved of you as My chosen instrument],
And before you were born I consecrated you [to Myself as My own];
I have appointed you as a prophet to the nations."
Then I said, "Ah, Lord God!
Behold, I do not know how to speak,
For I am [only] a young man."
But the Lord said to me,
"Do not say, 'I am [only] a young man,'
Because everywhere I send you, you shall go,
And whatever I command you, you shall speak."

JEREMIAH 1:5–7

*L*oving and serving her Lord was her destiny. Gwendolyn Ruth had parents who dedicated her to the Lord from the womb. She was born to serve the Lord.

Gwen's mother came from a godly family of sincere Mennonites who had served the Lord for many generations. These God-fearing forefathers paid a terrible price for their testimony. Years earlier these new believers were banished from their beautiful homes in the Emmental Valley of the Swiss Alps because of their conviction that salvation was by grace.

The teachings of Martin Luther had swept across Europe and changed their lives forever. Many of the faithful died as martyrs, being burned at the stake or speared through. Young men were sold as galley slaves, and old fathers were left to die in dark dungeons.

Gwen's ancestors were forced to leave their homes and live a life of wandering for decades until Russia opened its doors. There they found what they desired more than anything else: religious freedom.[1]

When all seemed to be going well, the Lord visited His people and warned them through the gift of prophecy that great persecution was coming to Russia. This persecution would be greater than any they had ever known in the past, and for those who stayed there would be no survivors. God told them to leave Russia and go to a new homeland. Some heeded the word of the Lord, while others mocked it and were left behind. Sadly, these endured unspeakable suffering and death. This is how Gwen came to be born in Canada.

During her teenage years, after a few months of rebellion and desperate prayers by her family, Gwen came back to the Lord and was gloriously filled with the Holy Spirit. She then went off to the Assembly of God Bible School in Ontario (Pentecostal Assemblies of Canada) to be trained for the Lord's work.

At school, revival fire fell among the students, and in the midst of this outpouring God called Gwen to China. Visions, spiritual gifts, intercession, and deep conviction of the Lord's presence flowed freely during those special days. But, somewhat ignorantly, Gwen had married a young man who was not as fervent about God's purposes. Gwen prayed and prayed. Eventually the Lord moved on his heart, and so in obedience they went off as faith missionaries to a distant land.

Gwen launched out to the mission field of China as a very young woman. It was December, 1947, when she landed in Shanghai, just having turned twenty-three years old. In obedience, she answered the call of God upon her life and received a passionate burden from the Lord for the Chinese people.

Sometimes that burden was greater than at other times. As the years went by and China fell into the hands of Communism, the doors for the gospel in mainland China slammed shut. Even so, Gwen continued to serve the Lord among the Chinese people in Taiwan and Hong Kong, not missing a step in fulfilling that call of God. Never for a moment did she think of turning back from that call. This dear pioneer loved the Chinese, and she considered them her people. She often stated, "I belonged to them, and their need was my need; their pain, my pain."[2]

But when circumstances changed in China, she went to India. She often would say, "China was my first love, and India was my great love."[3] No words could describe what it meant to feel God's heartbeat of love for a nation. She would have gladly laid down her whole life for the Lord in India. In fact, that became her desire.

In this season of her life, she experienced one of the greatest joys of service to God. Gwen raised a tent in many parts of northern India and openly preached the gospel of the Lord Jesus Christ as a woman on the front lines. What joy to see people respond to the mercy of God! How exciting to lead many Hindu and Muslim people to the Lord Jesus Christ!

After India, she traveled to Russia, where she became the first woman to preach at the Baptist church in Moscow. Her steps took her throughout northern Europe and she touched down in Africa. If she could pronounce the name of a place, Jesus took this little Canadian lady there. He introduced her to kings and princesses, paupers and lepers, and she shared with all the timeless story of God's great grace and wonderful love.

Her next call came and she went to Argentina where once again she felt the heartbeat of God, now for the Spanish-speaking people of that great land. Throughout Argentina she saw the mighty hand of God working with mighty displays of supernatural power following the preaching of His Word.

Then one night in Buenos Aires, something happened that was destined to change many lives. Gwen had just ministered in a large Assembly of God church where God had poured out His Spirit. Miracles of healing had taken place, and people had seen angels. God's tangible, manifested presence had come down to be among them. No one wanted to leave the meetings as the God of the secret place was now being revealed openly.

When Gwen went back tired and exhausted to the lonely hotel room that night, she lay there on her bed. Looking up to God, she asked Him a question. "God, how can you use me? I am nothing. I make mistakes. I am far from perfect. Yet I have seen your glory like a trail of fire following me everywhere. How? Why?"

An amazing thing happened; He answered! "It's because you are willing to do anything I ask you to do!" With the curiosity of a child, Gwen inquired, "Is that all, Lord? Then you could use anyone, any woman, who like myself would be totally surrendered to you."

"Yes, my child, I could," He answered.

Strengthened in faith, Gwen responded, "Then, Lord, raise up ten thousand women—women just like myself who will pay any price, make any sacrifice, and be totally obedient to your will."[4] The year was 1966 when this cry of birthing was heard in the night.

With fresh resolve, faith, and obedience, Gwen began to give the call to women everywhere to join her in sharing her burden for souls. A living organism was born—one full of consecration, holiness, and the Word of the Lord. The End-Time Handmaidens rose up from nation to nation as the Holy Spirit prepared women's hearts around the world in the same way He had prepared hers.

Reflect & Pray

1. If you could go to any country in the world to share the gospel, which country would you choose? Why?

2. Do you personally know a missionary? What is that person's life like compared to yours?

3. If you know a missionary, is this person happy with his or her life? Why or why not?

4. What do you think the greatest drawback would be if you were a missionary? How do you think God would help you overcome this drawback?

Lord God of all nations, thank you for the missionaries who risk harm to spread your Word to those who may have never heard about Jesus Christ. Please give me the courage to obey your calling no matter where you may lead me. In Jesus' name, amen.

To Know Christ:
Elizabeth Alves

"These signs will accompany those who have believed: in
My name they will cast out demons, they will speak in new
tongues; they will pick up serpents, and if they drink anything
deadly, it will not hurt them; they will lay hands on the sick,
and they will get well."

MARK 16:17–18

"I never wanted a ministry. All I ever wanted was to know Christ!"
These words epitomize the heart and motive of our dear friend
and another intimate friend of the secret place, Beth Alves.

When you're sitting in a meeting listening to Beth speak, you
might easily feel as if you're being ushered into her living room. Her
mothering grace is calm and unassuming. Here is a woman who
has traveled to over thirty nations speaking with rich and poor, to
rulers and peasants, always faithfully bringing the life of Christ to
countless thousands. Nevertheless, Beth Alves exudes the simplicity of those who love God. She knows that all her accomplishments
are not really hers but belong to Him, her beautiful Jesus.

Beth remembers a pivotal time within her family that was key
to their spiritual awakening. Her daughter had been diagnosed
with an inoperable brain tumor. As Beth watched her daughter
become increasingly debilitated, she prayed night and day. Walking
the floors, she pleaded, "Jesus, if you're the same yesterday, today,
and forever and if I called you and you would walk this floor, then
you would heal my daughter." Finally, Beth's daughter got to the
point at which she could no longer talk or swallow. She no longer

recognized her father—her favorite person. The only person she did know was Beth.

One day Beth came into her daughter's room in the hospital and busied herself because she was so depressed. As she started to clean the bedside table drawer, she pulled out a Gideon Bible and opened it, longing for something special to read. Growing up in the church, she had learned many wonderful Bible stories, but she didn't really know the Bible. At the time, she thought that was what the preacher was paid for—to study the Bible and preach from it.

Beth loved the Lord, but just didn't know much about Him. Opening up the Bible, she uttered a prayer of desperation asking for something special from Him. As she turned the pages, she found a Scripture that said, "He who believes and is baptized will be saved; but he who does not believe will be condemned. And these signs will follow those who believe: In My name they will cast out demons" (Mark 16:16–17 NKJV).

Oh, Beth thought, *It's not Halloween. I certainly don't need that!*

"They will speak with new tongues."

She looked at her daughter and thought, *I can't go to another country and learn a new tongue right now. I've got to take care of her here and now.*

"They will take up serpents."

Now, God, you know that I'm afraid of snakes. I'd never do that!

"And if they drink anything deadly, it will by no means hurt them" (see Mark 16: 17–18).

Finally Beth's eyes fell on a part of the passage that would change her life forever. Slowly, absorbing every word, she read, "they will lay hands on the sick, and they will recover" (Mark 16:18 NKJV).

Aha! That's exactly what she needed! Beth laid the open Bible across her daughter's feet, as if she were showing God what He had written. Carefully, tentatively placing her hands on the dying child's feet, Beth looked up to heaven and declared aloud: "God, I'm doing it. It doesn't say pray. Here it says to lay hands on them."

Feeling a little more hopeful, she closed the Bible and finished cleaning out the drawer. The next morning her daughter had another pneumoencephalogram test. Beth had no guarantee her daughter would come out alive.

The doctors emerged from the testing room with tears running down their faces. Panic filled her heart; Beth was afraid she had lost her daughter. They took Beth's daughter to her room still under the anesthetic. Setting next to her emaciated daughter, Beth's hot tears rolled down her face and splashed onto her lap, soaking her dress.

As if dreaming, suddenly she heard, "Hey Mom, where's Daddy? I'm hungry—let's eat." Beth's daughter was sitting up in bed, completely healed!

"Lord, teach me to pray," became Beth's desperate cry in those early days. God faithfully answered her prayer. Over the years, the Lord has unfolded to Beth simple yet profound truths about prayer and intercession that she continues to impart to others. Thousands from many nations have been released into ministry as they have learned principles of prayer and prophecy. With gentleness, humor, and simplicity, she captures the hearts of her listeners, encouraging them that they, too, can hear the voice of the Lord.

In 1971, Beth sensed the Lord impressing upon her the importance of praying for spiritual leaders worldwide. Her vision was based on Isaiah 62:6–7. Beth and her husband Floyd founded Intercessors International in 1972. Here Beth has used her rich insights about prayer as a wonderful tool to shield leaders under a cover of loving, spiritual intercession. The Lord has taught Beth to pray, giving her much wisdom and extremely practical applications.

She has been called the "Grandma of the Prayer Shield." She has received great understanding about the need for our leaders to be covered in prayer. These leaders include ministers, missionaries, and business and spiritual leaders around the world. She teaches on many different types of intercessors, and with her great insight she is able to extend grace to others to flow in their own individually-tailored intercessory gifts.

Beth highly values the importance of godly mentoring. While her children were still young and at home, she turned down a significant opportunity from the Lord to start a prayer ministry. She felt it necessary to mentor her children and passed that opportunity onto another, believing that if the call truly was from God it would still be there when her children were grown. It was.

She has traveled extensively, teaching and ministering in seminars and conferences worldwide. She has participated in the March for Jesus in Berlin, Germany; her ministry was involved in "The Concert for the Lord in the Heart of the Gobi Desert," and in Romania as they prayed about the injustices committed against the children. She has great proficiency and accuracy in delivering prophetic ministry, which has given her great credibility among world leaders. Beth is also well-known in Germany where she and Floyd lived as missionaries.

Beth has authored a number of books including: *Becoming a Prayer Warrior, The Mighty Warrior: A Guide to Effective Prayer, Daily Prayers,* and booklets in the *Praying with Purpose* series. She also co-authored *Intercessors: Discover Your Prayer Power.*

Reflect & Pray

1. Studying the Bible gives you power to overcome every challenge. What are some challenges you are confronting that you need His power to face?

2. Do you believe that God heals physically broken bodies today? Why or why not?

3. If you believe that God heals today, yesterday, and tomorrow, why do you think people are still suffering?

4. Take time to say a prayer for those you know who are burdened with physical challenges.

Father, teach me to pray. Let your will be done, your kingdom come. There is so much information in this world, Father. But I don't want just information; I want that which will bring life to your people, in the name of Jesus, and I give you the praise, honor, and glory in Jesus' name, amen.

Day 26

Going to the Cross

Blessed and greatly favored are those who dwell in
Your house and Your presence; They will be singing
Your praises all the day long. Selah.

PSALM 84:4

O f all the men and women in the Bible who came to know God intimately, David was certainly one who understood what it meant to enter the secret place of the Holy Spirit. In Psalm 84, David paints a sensitive and inviting word picture for us:

How lovely are Your dwelling places, O LORD of hosts! My soul (my life, my inner self) longs for and greatly desires the courts of the LORD; My heart and my flesh sing for joy to the living God. The bird has found a house, And the swallow a nest for herself, where she may lay her young— Even Your altars, O LORD of hosts, My King and my God. Blessed and greatly favored are those who dwell in Your house and Your presence; They will be singing Your praises all the day long. Selah. ... Passing through the Valley of Weeping (Baca), they make it a place of springs; The early rain also covers it with blessings. They go from strength to strength [increasing in victorious power]; Each of them appears before God in Zion. ... For a day in Your courts is better than a thousand [anywhere else]; I would rather stand [as a doorkeeper] at the threshold of the house of my God Than to live [at ease] in the tents of wickedness. (Psalm 84:1–4, 6–7,10)

Recently when I read this wonderful psalm, I was in a quiet and reflective mood with the Lord. I felt Him drawing my attention to verse three: "Yes, the sparrow has found a house, and the swallow a nest for herself, where she may lay her young—even Your altars, O Lord of hosts, my King and my God."

This Scripture is one of my most treasured possessions. It was treasured by my grandmother and then by my mother. It has become part of my family heritage. The more Scripture we have hidden away in our hearts, the greater the opportunity we give God to speak into our beings. I have one such experience I'd like to share with you.

My girls and I were over at our neighbor's place where they were taking riding lessons. As the horses were being brought in, groomed, and saddled up, I was enjoying myself by watching everyone and all the animals. I happened to look up and see a barn swallow's nest built against the rafters of the barn. *What a delightful find!* I thought.

My excitement was genuine, for my mother had been quite a bird-watcher and had taught me to highly value these beautiful creatures for their unique qualities.

Personally, I think that barn swallows are some of the most beautiful birds in God's creation. They have such an iridescent bluish-black coloring on their backs, and their faces, throats, and breasts are rich shades of deep orange. These precious little creatures perform like flying acrobats as they swoop and dive after insects in the early evening light.

As I stood there admiring these fascinating little birds, the Lord began to weave together for me an understanding of Psalm 84 using these beautiful swallows. I found myself thinking what an accurate picture David had painted concerning their nature, especially when building their nests.

A swallow will first find a structure where there is a supply of mud close by. It will carry mud and twigs in its little beak, making trip after trip. Then it carefully constructs its nest, placing the mud on a board up close to the ceiling of the barn, creating a mud-dauber type of structure. The outside of the nest is very solid and very secure. Yet the inside of the nest is lined with down feathers and is soft, warm, and inviting.

There is an understanding of the way of wisdom that God has deposited within His creation. In animals we call it "instinct." How do the birds know to fly south for the winter? Where do they get their sense of when it is time to start their migration? How do they know which way to go, covering hundreds of miles every year? They don't deal with fears or "the flesh." They were created with the knowing that these things are the right and safe things to do.

The thought struck me: *Swallows build their nests the way they do because, instinctively, they know that the safest place to build is up against the wall.* On the other hand, we use the expression "up against the wall" to describe a place of inner struggle where we may feel trapped or feel that we've run out of options, and we have no place to run and no way out.

As human beings, we don't have instinct deposited within us apart from the Holy Spirit. Instead, God leaves us to make our choices, having shown us in His Word the narrow road to follow. Our mistakes and failures have left scars of fear and anxiety which cause us to think running away will keep us safe. Oh, that we would learn from the swallow the wisdom of God, that we would let our Divine Shepherd's leading and guiding become so deep in us so as to mirror the powerful instincts built within His creation. May He build within the fabric of our lives the truth that the place of abiding is found where difficulty crosses our will and our fear. That is actually the safest place.

To quote an old and wise saying: "Going to the cross is going to the point where my will crosses God's will." How desperately we need to abide in God by staying close to the cross!

Each one of us must go to the cross. There are no exceptions. The cross is the place where our will and God's will cross each other. The cross is always the place where God's will stands before me, the place I want to run from as fast and far as I can. But you see, that's the point where God will meet us—where we are spiritually weakest. It's also the point at which He will give us His grace and strength in place of our weakness.

Too often we wait until difficulty comes, and we frantically try to throw together a nest—a piece of homespun philosophy here, what Oprah said there—anything to grasp at security. It's like the flimsy little nest I discovered on two dead branches outside our office. Some of us even convince ourselves that we're doing OK all on our own. What we've latched onto seems good, but there is a big problem—the nests of security we build out of what the world has to offer are not anchored. They offer no real security, only the illusion of it. When the wind comes, that flimsy little nest will fall. Security of our own making grants us no real abiding place.

If you get quiet enough and listen, you'll hear Him calling you too. Yes, the sparrow has found a house and the swallow a nest for herself. David and so many others found their rest at the altars of the Lord. And now it's your turn. Softly, tenderly, quietly He's calling you from the depths of His wonderful presence. How will you respond? Will you join Him in the secret place?

Reflect & Pray

1. Do you have a favorite psalm? If so, write it and allow God to speak to you as you write each word. If not, prayerfully look through the book of Psalms and allow God to choose one for you. Then write the words.

2. Think about the last time you were pushed up "against the wall." Did you reach out to God for help or try to handle it on your own? Why?

3. "Going to the cross is going to the point where my will crosses God's will." When has this happened in your life?

4. Where have you built your nest? How secure are you in knowing that your nest is built in the safest place possible?

Dear heavenly Father, I come to you in the name of Jesus, your Son. I am longing to enter a deeper place of fellowship with you, but I'm not quite sure I know how to get there. Help me find my secret place to meet with you. Help me open up the room in my heart that is meant for only you and me together, forever! Let me hear the song you are singing over the mountains, trying to reach my heart. Give me the song to sing that will so bless your heart, and bring you great joy. Lord, come, and take all the bits and pieces of my life and my heart, and make them into a beautiful symphony of love of devotion to you! I love you! In Jesus' name, amen.

Day 27
A Pilgrim's Progress

[I always pray] that the God of our Lord Jesus Christ,
the Father of glory, may grant you a spirit of wisdom and
of revelation [that gives you a deep and personal and intimate
insight] into the true knowledge of Him [for we know
the Father through the Son] And [I pray] that the eyes of
your heart [the very center and core of your being] may be
enlightened [flooded with light by the Holy Spirit], so that
you will know and cherish the hope [the divine guarantee,
the confident expectation] to which He has called you, the
riches of His glorious inheritance in the saints (God's people),
and [so that you will begin to know] what the immeasurable
and unlimited and surpassing greatness of His
[active, spiritual] power is in us who believe. These are
in accordance with the working of His mighty strength.

EPHESIANS 1:17–19

Like Christian in *Pilgrim's Progress,* God is taking me on a journey. When I found myself in the valley of intimidation, He introduced me to a "hall of heroes" like the ones described by the prophet Nehemiah and the writer of the Book of Hebrews. (See Nehemiah 7 and Hebrews 11.)

First, He introduced me to many heroines of courage and I was drawn to and immersed in the life of Joan of Arc. She taught me that the darkness of the age we live in does not really matter because God's light is eternal, and He will open every door for us if we truly love Him and desire for His will to be done. As a result, my heart became a flame of passion that filled me with the courage I needed to sever the chains of intimidation that had held me captive for so long; and my appetite for more of God became truly insatiable!

Next, I began to devour books about other great women of faith and courage: Vibia Perpetua, Sojourner Truth, Harriet Tubman, Aimee Semple McPherson, Lydia Prince, Bertha Smith, Corrie ten Boom, and Jackie Pullinger. I wrote about these great women—the foundation of my own hall of heroes—in *A Call to Courage,* and we have looked at them together now.

As I built upon that foundation and continued walking through the hallway, my heart became even more on-fire, and I fell more deeply in love with my heavenly Father, who began helping me to build the second level of my hall of heroes. The Lord gave me fresh insights and showed me how He had always been with me even during the most trying times of my life. I know that He will always be with me!

Through the writings of Madame Jeanne Guyon I received further spiritual enlightenment and new understandings of God and His ways. Her profound wisdom helped me to firmly establish Jesus as the center of my life; when this happened, everything in my life began to fall into place and I discovered a wonderfully deep peace in Him. This brought great healing and strength to my soul.

As I continued on, I studied the lives of Teresa of Avila, Susanna Wesley, Fanny Crosby, Basilea Schlink, Gwen Shaw, and Elizabeth Alves. Oh, the riches I learned from these special women. Like Susanna Wesley, I determined that my prayer closet would become my apron. I basked in the anointing that rested upon the famous blind hymn writer Fanny Crosby, whose inspiring and stirring hymns ushered in a vital spiritual awakening in her time and continue to minister personally to people everywhere.

These new "friends" of mine—those we have just looked at— were brought together in my second book in the *Women on the Front Lines* series, entitled *A Call to the Secret Place.* This book has released a sweet fragrance of God that I deeply cherish and wish to spread wherever I go.

As a result of all that God has shown me through these experiences and intense study, I am now convinced that if we have truly experienced the transformation that always occurs when we abide in His presence it will cause us to turn outward to bring this powerful transformation to the world. After all, this is the power of the love of God that we have known and experienced. His heart is always reaching out to anyone who will receive Him.

If I have truly been set free from fear and intimidation and have been filled with a courageous spirit, and if I have truly found my resting place in the heart of God, I must continue on this journey and move my heart to act on behalf of others. This is something I must embrace, and it requires me to get out of my chair and begin walking with the feet He surely gave me for this purpose. In other words, I must stir myself to action.

Therefore, I've looked into the lives of other women who have known this same compelling call and have forged a trail that we must follow. These trailblazers are Catherine Booth, Nancy Ward, Florence Nightingale, Gladys Aylward, Mother Teresa, Heidi Baker, and a whole company of other women. These ladies have challenged the systems of their day and met life, circumstances, and even governments with attitudes of gutsy determination that flew in the face of and blasted anything that resisted God's love and power.

I love these women. Their don't-tell-me-I-can't determination is what I want for my own life and for your life as well. With them, I'm committed to continue my journey, and I want to bring as many men and women who desire to love the Lord with all their hearts and to love their neighbors as themselves along with me.

Now I have a few questions for you. What is your heart telling you? Do you want to break open whole regions of the earth for the

Lord's heart? Do you want to make a difference in someone's life? Do you want to break off and break out of the limitations that have bound you up and paralyzed you? Then come along with me. Join me on this exciting journey.

Let's build a whole company of "laid-down lovers" for Jesus' sake, as Heidi Baker would say. The Father is waiting for us to fill His house. He is waiting and longing for you and me to take action.

Reflect & Pray

1. What is your heart telling you about God's call for your life?
2. What part of the world do you want to see impacted?
3. Name one person you want to influence for Jesus' sake?
4. What limitations do you want to be free of so that you can walk in freedom?

Dear God, may I gain strength from your Word, your voice, and the women who were committed to bringing your kingdom on earth as it is in heaven. Thank you for these strong women who were empowered by your faithfulness. In Jesus' name, amen.

Day 28

In Tune with God's Heart

He has told you, O man, what is good; And what does
the Lord require of you Except to be just, and to love [and
to diligently practice] kindness (compassion), And to walk
humbly with your God [setting aside any overblown
sense of importance or self-righteousness]?

MICAH 6:8

On a trip to Thailand I found myself in a Mexican restaurant in Bangkok. The young ladies who worked as servers were wearing cowboy hats, cowboy boots, and other Western wear. I thought it was really funny to see such outfits in Bangkok, never mind in a "Mexican" restaurant!

My friends and I were having a delightful conversation—a nice respite from our hectic schedule of prayer meetings, travel, sleeping in different hotels, and many, many meetings. As I looked around the room, I noticed a young man who was standing outside. He was holding a sign, and he had several little toys dangling on fine strings all around him.

From the booth where we were sitting, I noticed his sign read that he was deaf and he had created these little toys, which were crickets, out of bits of bamboo. He was selling them for a modest price of twenty *baht* (approximately fifty cents) apiece so he could buy food.

Though he was a simple and needy young man, he didn't look like he was begging. He stood upright, showed no emotion, and did not really try to sell me anything. He did not have the typical pleading eyes of a beggar, and he did not gesture for my attention.

I was impressed by how he stood with an air of quiet self-respect and seeming uprightness of heart. I will never forget the look I saw in his eyes. We did not exchange a word between us, but our hearts touched each other that day as we peered into each other's souls. I believe I gave him something that day—something far more than the twenty *baht* it cost me to buy a cricket. I gave him my promise to do all I could with my life to make a difference in his life and in the lives of others like him.

At the same time he gave me something, something I desperately needed. He gave me the privilege of touching his life, of making a difference. I caught a glimpse into the heart of God. This young man showed me that you don't have to be somebody who is important or famous—you just have to be available. You have to be willing to engage in the journey and walk the path that Jesus walks every day. This is what the journey of learning God's ways is all about.

Whenever I look at my little cricket I bought from this young man, I remember this treasured experience, and I renew my commitment to the Lord Jesus Christ. Thus, I continue on the journey that has been set before me.

Do you want more of Jesus? Is your heart engaged with the things that move His heart? Do you want more of the Father's love deposited in your heart? How can we understand this amazing love that He so deeply desires for us to experience? His love is beyond our mental abilities to comprehend.

Many of us have tainted understandings of what a father is like. Our understanding of fatherhood is shaped by our childhood experiences with our earthly fathers. So, we have to ask ourselves, "What do I really know about God and His heart? What do I really know about His mercy and compassion?" To know His mercy and compassion, we must open our hearts to Him. We must go to the place where He exposes the tenderness of His heart—the written Word.

True compassion and mercy stem from a passion for the Father's heart. Do you love mercy? When we learn to truly love mercy and compassion, out of our passion for God's heart we will be motivated to act justly.

Justice and righteousness form the foundation of the Father's throne. The psalmist wrote, "Righteousness and justice are the foundation of Your throne; Lovingkindness and truth go before You" (Psalm 89:14).

Go to God's throne of grace as we begin and ask Him for an impartation of grace and a spirit of revelation to come upon you. Ask God to enlighten your mind and to fill your heart with His fire. Open your heart to the Holy Spirit and let Him speak to you, guide you, teach you, and move you. Let the river of God, which is always full, flow forth in all its energy and power.

Did you ever consider the fact that happiness comes from walking in compassion? This is what David meant when he wrote, "Blessed [by God's grace and compassion] is he who considers the helpless; The LORD will save him in the day of trouble" (Psalm 41:1). What a glorious promise this is!

These are just some of the things that happen when we are filled with compassion and reach out in love to others. Doesn't this make you want to really be in tune with God's heart as you begin your journey?

God's compassions never fail. In fact, they are renewed every day (see Lamentations 3:22–23). He wants us to keep our hearts open to Him each day as well. We must be careful to guard against any bitterness or hardness of heart that may try to creep into our lives. God actually commands us to never let our hearts and minds grow hard or cold (see Deuteronomy 15:7–10).

What does God want from us? Open hands and open hearts and a willingness to help those in need. He wants us to give freely and cheerfully. This is mercy in action, the love of God reaching out to the oppressed.

True justice involves both kindness and compassion. Zechariah wrote:

> Thus has the LORD of hosts said, 'Dispense true justice and practice kindness and compassion, to each other; and do not oppress *or* exploit the widow or the fatherless, the stranger or the poor; and do not devise *or* even imagine evil in your hearts against one another.' (Zechariah 7:9-10)

Do you see the relationship between justice and compassion that is portrayed here? In order to understand God's plumb line of justice we have to know what He values. On a trip to Mozambique the Lord showed me something I had never seen before and as He did so He said to me, "Mercy without justice enables thievery!"

We need to understand what mercy and compassion are according to God's standards, not according to the standards of secular humanism. From His point of view, compassion must always involve justice.

Reflect & Pray

1. What is your initial reaction to seeing beggars on the street? Would your reaction be different if you were in a foreign country? Why?

2. How have you had the privilege of touching other people's lives by helping supply their needs?

3. "Happiness comes from walking in compassion." How has showing compassion to others brought happiness in your life?

4. What does it mean that "compassion must always involve justice"?

Dear God of all justice and mercy, thank you for being a righteous Judge who is merciful and forgiving. May I always remember your love for me when I repent and seek your forgiveness for my sins. In Jesus' name, amen.

Day 29

Justice, Righteousness,
and Compassion

He who oppresses the poor taunts and
insults his Maker, But he who is kind and merciful
and gracious to the needy honors Him.

PROVERBS 14:31

God wants governments to rule with justice, righteousness, and compassion, but we all know that this is not always the case. The psalmist wrote:

God stands in the divine assembly;
He judges among the gods (divine beings). How long will
you judge unjustly And show partiality to the wicked?
Selah. Vindicate the weak and fatherless;
Do justice *and* maintain the rights of the afflicted and
destitute. Rescue the weak and needy; Rescue them from
the hand of the wicked. (Psalm 82:1–4)

Here we see God's heart concerning true judicial government. Such a government should not show partiality and it should always do justice to the poor, the fatherless, the afflicted, and the needy. In fact, it should even deliver the poor and needy and rescue them from the wicked.

As followers of Jesus, we should do everything within our power to make sure that this is the kind of government we have. We should vote for godly candidates, and we should vote the wicked out of office. God might even call us to run for public office ourselves so that His justice, righteousness, and mercy can take hold where we live. It is time to stand up in the seats of government and let our lights shine!

The following Scripture shook me to the core of my being as its truth penetrated my spirit: "He who oppresses the poor taunts and insults his Maker, But he who is kind and merciful and gracious to the needy honors Him" (Proverbs 14:31). I don't know how this could be any clearer.

I would like to think of myself as a righteous person, but there have been many, many times when I've had to repent of my lack of mercy and my unwillingness to tune my heart to God's heart.

My desire is to be like the woman who is described in Proverbs 31:20: "She opens and extends her hand to the poor, And she reaches out her filled hands to the needy." This verse speaks volumes to me, for it shows a righteous woman in action.

I once had a dream in which I saw twenty or thirty people standing all around me. It seemed that they had been witnesses of my life. One particular man who was standing over me had a spirit of prophecy resting on him. He reminded me of an old-fashioned water pump, the kind where you prime the pump first and then start moving the handle up and down. I sensed that, as this man moved from side to side, the water of God's Word was building up inside of him.

In this dream I was very sick. My body was crumpled over an old stone wall, and I was crying, "Will someone get me a doctor? I'm very, very sick!"

Everybody stared at me, and the man I mentioned said, "Don't you know you've been called to prayer and fasting?"

I said, "I need help. Will someone please get me a doctor?"

Again he said, "Don't you know you've been called to prayer and fasting?"

I whimpered, "Please! Somebody help me! Please! I need help!"

The man stood in front of me and repeated, "Don't you know you've been called to prayer and fasting?" Then he added: "Don't you know that if you would enter into prayer and fasting, you would extend the orphan's bread from three to five days?"

This question hit me hard. I began to see that what I needed was not a doctor after all. What I really needed was to obey the Lord by entering into a place of prayer and fasting.

I'm terrible at fasting. I really am. Fasting represents a monumental struggle with my flesh. I really have a hard time with it. God's chosen fast, however, goes beyond the issue of food and flesh; it goes deep into your heart.

God's chosen fast becomes a lifestyle that we are called to embrace. What is His chosen fast? The Bible tells us: "[Rather] is this not the fast which I choose, To undo the bonds of wickedness, To tear to pieces the ropes of the yoke, To let the oppressed go free And break apart every [enslaving] yoke?" (Isaiah 58:6). Now that's a powerful fast!

Have you entered a fast that divides your bread with the hungry? Have you brought the homeless into your home, covered the naked, and provided for the needs of your family and all those around you? (See Isaiah 58:7.)

This is God's chosen fast, and it is truly an exciting fast in which to get engaged, for this is always its result:

Then your light will break out like the dawn, And your healing (restoration, new life) will quickly spring forth; Your righteousness will go before you [leading you to peace and prosperity], The glory of the LORD will be your rear guard. (Isaiah 58:8)

I don't know about you, but I'll sure take that. This is God's chosen fast for you and me.

Jesus always saw the need first, then He was moved with a compassion so strong that it always led Him to do something in response to the need. Matthew wrote, "When He saw the crowds, He was moved with compassion and pity for them, because they were dispirited and distressed, like sheep without a shepherd" (Matthew 9:36).

If you have compassion, you will be moved to take action as Jesus always was and is. God wants you to know His compassion, receive His compassion, live His compassion, and share His compassion with others.[1]

Compassion will move so deeply within your being that many times you will find yourself moved to the point of tears and agony. Ah, this is a beautiful place. God places great value in your tears and as we turn to the next chapter, you will discover this is a deep well which moves heaven on behalf of others.

Reflect & Pray

1. In your own words, write what you believe is God's view of true judicial government.
2. "God's chosen fast, however, goes beyond the issue of food and flesh; it goes deep into your heart." What has your experience been with fasting?
3. What is the difference between compassion and pity?
4. Has compassion for others moved you to tears or agony? Reflect on that experience.

Heavenly Father, I come to you right now in the name of Jesus. Light the fire of passion in my life and let it become the kind of compassion that doesn't just look at the need, but looks to you. Help me to become so passionate for loving you and knowing your heart that I will move in compassion to all those in need. I ask that you will bring about a corporate shift of thinking and acting in the entire body of Christ, that your people would become passionate about compassion by being passionate for you. I cry out to you, Father, and ask that you would take the Scriptures I've read in this chapter and drop their truths deep within my heart. Let your Word continue to flow within the depths of my spirit so I will be able to receive all the spiritual nutrients you have for me. Drop your plumb line of justice through all of my thoughts and feelings, all of my traditions and training, and let me learn to do justly and to love mercy and to walk humbly with you. In Jesus' name, amen.

Day 30

The Power of Tears

> As He approached Jerusalem, He saw the city and wept
> over it [and the spiritual ignorance of its people], saying,
> "If [only] you had known on this day [of salvation], even
> you, the things which make for peace [and on which peace
> depends]! But now they have been hidden from your eyes.
>
> LUKE 19:41–42

*W*hen Jesus saw the throngs of people who were suffering as a result of their sins, He was moved with compassion for them. Often, He even wept over them. The shortest verse in the Bible says, "Jesus wept" (John 11:35). What was He weeping over here? First, He saw the need, which was the death of Lazarus.

Then He heard the cry of Martha's heart: "Lord, if You had been here, my brother would not have died" (John 11:21). At this point Martha expressed her faith in the Master's ability to heal. She said, "And even now I know that whatever You ask from God, God will give it to You" (John 11:22).

Next, Jesus heard the piercing cries of Mary, the sister of Martha and Lazarus, and "When Jesus saw her sobbing, and the Jews who had come with her also sobbing, He was deeply moved in spirit [to the point of anger at the sorrow caused by death] and was troubled" (John 11:33).

Because He saw and listened actively to the heart-cries of Martha, Mary, and the assembled Jews and was tuned in to the resonance of the heart of Father God Himself, Jesus was *moved with compassion* and in turn ministered effectively to the urgent need at hand. John the beloved describes in detail how Lazarus came forth from the tomb—he bolted forth, demonstrating the power of the resurrection from the dead. Tears preceded this power encounter. Perhaps compassion and power are inevitably linked.

Yes, our tears have the power to cleanse, to enable us to see, and to thrust us to action on behalf of those in need.

As we hear God speaking to our hearts, we need to obey His inner promptings. As good parents raising their children frequently say, "Just listen and obey!" Obedience brings action to our feelings. Obedience demonstrates commitment to our inner convictions and moves us beyond ourselves.

Jesus was frequently moved with pity, sympathy, and compassion for the people He saw around Him. He really saw them, and He saw their needs. This means He was fully aware, perceptive, understanding, and responsive to them.

> Often the Lord saw people as being bewildered, like sheep without a shepherd, and this deeply troubled Him, as we see in the Gospel of Mark, "When Jesus went ashore, He saw a large crowd [waiting], and He was moved with compassion for them because they were like sheep without a shepherd [lacking guidance]; and He began to teach them many things" (Mark 6:34).

It has been accurately said that when a need is presented to us we really have three options:

- To be *inactive*—to do nothing. Like the proverbial ostrich, we can choose to stick our heads in the sand and hope the problem will go away.
- To be *reactive*—this is an emotional response, usually in the form of anger, to a troubling situation.
- To be *proactive*—this involves taking positive steps to rectify the problem.

Jesus, when He was moved with compassion, was always proactive. In the case just cited in the Scripture, we see that He responded to the disorientation He saw in the people by commanding kingdom order and thus teaching them to rule and reign in life.

As we go forth in compassion, we need to do more than just express sympathy or pity. As Jesus did, we need to do something concrete to help others. Perhaps the best help we can give others is to teach them how to overcome through faith, prayer, and spiritual understanding. We need to exemplify kingdom authority right out in the open as Jesus did for all to see. The kind of compassion Jesus walked in was not weak and passive; it was tender yet tough, sensitive yet confrontational.

David wrote, "The sacrifices of God are a broken spirit; a broken and contrite heart, O God, you will not despise" (Psalm 51:17 NIV).

The great evangelist and writer Charles Finney knew and practiced the truth of this verse. He had a weeping heart. He often went into the woods north of his village to pray and he confessed that he did this so that others would not see him. He wrote:

> An overwhelming sense of my wickedness in being ashamed to have a human being see me on my knees before God took such a powerful possession of me that I cried at the top of my voice, and I exclaimed that I would not leave, and I proclaimed that I would not leave this place, that if all the men on earth, and all the devils in hell surrounded me. I prayed until my mind became so full that before I was aware of it I was on my feet and tripping up the ascent towards the road.[1]

Though he had gone into the woods at dawn, when he reached town it was already noon. He had been so lost in prayer that time had lost all meaning to him. He later went to dinner but discovered that he had no appetite for food, so he went to his office to play hymns on his bass viola, but he found that he couldn't sing without weeping. He shares what happened as that night progressed:

> All my feelings seemed to rise and to flow out, the utterance of my heart was, I want to pour out my whole soul to God. The rising of my soul was so great, I went … back to the front office to pray, I wept like a child, and made such confession as I could with my choked utterance. It seemed to be as though I bathed His feet with my tears.[2]

This weeping servant sowed precious seed into the lives of two and a half million people who came to know the Lord Jesus Christ as their personal Savior. Research tells us that at least 75 percent of these converts remained true to Christ till their deaths.

This is what we need today—men and women of God who learn the power of tears, the compassion of Christ, the importance of prayer, and the fire of the Holy Spirit.

Intercessory prayer combined with compassionate weeping is a powerful force that truly brings change in our world today. As William Booth declared, "Try tears!"

Do you want to move in compassion? Then receive compassion. Do you want to move in healing? Then receive healing. Do you want to move in deliverance? Then receive deliverance. Whatever you receive by faith through the love of God you will be authorized to give away.

Reflect & Pray

1. People usually weep as a reaction to seeing or experiencing something joyful, upsetting, or shocking. Think about the last time you cried. Was it prompted by self-focus or others-focus?

2. When you are presented with a need, are you more often inactive, reactive, or proactive? Why?

3. Have you ever been "lost in prayer"? If not, do you want to be? Why?

4. What does the power of tears mean to you?

Dear compassionate One, thank you for the insights of your faithful followers. May I learn from them and your holy Word how to be more compassionate and loving toward all of your children. In Jesus' name, amen.

Day 31

Trailblazer for Women: Catherine Booth (1829-1890)

Be kind and helpful to one another, tender-hearted
[compassionate, understanding], forgiving one another
[readily and freely], just as God in Christ also forgave you.

EPHESIANS 4:32

In 1878, William Booth declared his vision for the Salvation Army. He said, "To postpone action any further will be an act of disobedience to what we both sense is the divine will of God."

His wife Catherine was in full support of this declaration. She said, "William, don't hold back because of me. I can trust in God and go out with Him, and I can live on bread and water. Go out and do your duty. God will provide if we will only go straight on in the path of duty."

It was at this point that they broke with an established ministry affiliation and began their own independent evangelistic ministry. The distinguishing features of this ministry were authority, obedience, the adapted employment of everyone's abilities, the training and discipline of all workers, and the combined action of all.

They adapted army jargon in their work. William believed very much in the chain of command, and he became a general whose job was to oversee the ministry. They trained the people who worked with them and taught them how to endure and rise above the mocking of the crowds which sometimes occurred.

The idea of uniforms began to emerge at this point as well, and the bonnets for the women were designed in such a way as to protect them from rotten eggs and garbage that were sometimes thrown at them.

The Booths expected their workers to go into the most distressful situations and love the most needy, most hurting, and sometimes even the most hateful! They also believed in the importance of combining their forces like a mighty army as they reached out to those in need.

At this stage in their lives, William and Catherine Booth were only thirty-two years old. They had five children and very little money. They settled in Leeds, a town in the English midlands, and began to conduct separate campaigns so as to increase their effectiveness.

Hundreds of adults and children responded to the invitation to find Christ under Catherine's preaching ministry in south and west London. Her preaching, along with the success William was experiencing in his ministry to the poor, came to the notice of *The Revival,* England's premier evangelistic journal.

As a result, William was invited to preach in White Chapel in early 1865. White Chapel was a poor section in the notorious East End of London. He asked Catherine to preach there as well.

Soon thereafter, Catherine became aware of the Midnight Movement for Fallen Women, an agency that combined evangelism with social redemption. Her experience with this organization opened her eyes to the need for social concern to become a part of their ministry.

Catherine began to see a need to champion the cause of women, and she advocated for them to be placed in positions of responsibility and usefulness within the church. Through her preaching in the West End, she touched the hearts and lives of people who could help provide financial support for the struggling work William was doing in the East End.

When speaking publicly, Catherine never minced her words. She spoke with boldness and righteous indignation as she confronted the evils of her day. In so doing she made the comfortable less comfortable, and she even went so far as to accuse affluent Christians by saying that they were responsible for the sweatshops and the filthy working conditions in which women and children found themselves.

Once she made this statement: "It will be a happy day for England when Christian ladies transfer their sympathies from poodles and terriers to destitute and starving children."

The Booths created the East London Christian Revival Society, which became known as the East London Christian Mission, or more commonly the Christian Mission. This later became known as the Salvation Army. Catherine became the primary promoter of this ministry, while William continued to work among the poor in the East End.

What a team they were! Catherine was doing the preaching and raising the funds, and William was in the trenches, ministering to the needs of the poor.

Early on their children learned what ministry was all about. Their oldest child, William Bramwell Booth, was dedicated to God when he was born. Catherine said, "I held him up to God as soon as I had strength to do so, and I remember specially desiring that he should be an advocate of holiness." They had a total of eight children, and each one became active in the work of the Salvation Army.

Catherine Booth organized Food-for-the-Million shops where the poor could afford inexpensively priced hot soup and three-course dinners. On special occasions, such as Christmas, she would cook more than 300 dinners that were distributed to the poor.

By 1882 there were almost 17,000 people worshiping under the auspices of the Salvation Army, far more than the attendance in mainline churches. This caused the Archbishop of York, the Rev. Dr. William Thornton, to comment that the Salvation Army was reaching people that the Church of England had failed to reach.

Since those early days and more than a century later, the Salvation Army remains a vital force in the world. As a result of the Army's ministry, new laws protecting women and children were enacted in England. The impact of the Salvation Army has reached around the world, and its ministries include prison work, youth work, rescue homes for women, ministry to alcoholics and drug addicts, rescue missions, salvage operations, disaster relief, and men's hostels.

The Salvation Army has earned the respect of the White House, the United States Supreme Court and Congress, embassies worldwide, and governments in many nations.

Catherine Booth was the mother of the Salvation Army. She knew that compassion *acts,* and she also knew that it is born out of passion for the Father's heart. She wrote, "Don't let controversy hurt your soul. Live near to God by prayer. Just fall down at His feet and open your very soul before him, and throw yourself right into His arms."

Reflect & Pray

1. Catherine Booth was a full partner with her husband in founding an organization that is recognized around the world. What perception do you have about the Salvation Army?

2. The Salvation Army helps thousands of people every day worldwide. What do you think of the attacks against them for refusing to compromise their Christian mission?

3. What do you think of when you see and hear "bell-ringers" at Christmastime?

4. Reflect on this statement: "Empowering those less fortunate than you also gives you power." How can you empower others less fortunate than you?

Father God, thank you for the wonderful example of Catherine Booth. I also want to be a person of compassion, who falls at your feet and opens my soul before you. I throw myself into your arms, dear Father, and ask you to light the fire of passion in my heart, that I would be aflame with your love and go forth in compassion to those who need to know how much you love them. Let me become a true agent of change in the world as I act in mercy to others. May their lives be completely transformed by your grace and may they see that you truly are their Father. Give me your wisdom, Lord, so I can see things from your point of view. Help me not to lean upon my own insight, but to trust you for all things. As I acknowledge you, I know you will direct my path. Thank you, Father. In Jesus' name, amen.

Beloved Woman of the Cherokee: Nancy Ward (1738–1822)

I will praise and give thanks to You, O LORD, among
the people; I will sing praises to You among the nations.

PSALM 57:9

A fresh wind is blowing within the body of Christ. Across denominational, racial, and political lines the Spirit of God is exposing the roots of ritual-based Christian religion. This exposure is showing many of us ways in which our religious expressions have supplanted an authentic relationship with the fullness of the Father. Starting down this path of the revelation of our citizenship in God's kingdom, we begin to encounter many paradigms—paradigms that, for whatever reason, we may have chosen to ignore. Comfort in America is being displaced with a kind of holy unrest. It is in this place of holy unrest that we begin to collide with realities which are uncomfortable to look directly in the eye.

Native American societies lived in cooperation with their environment. This contrasts the ideals of exploitation versus stewardship. When Europeans arrived on the North American continent, they found a pristine environment with little impact from thousands of years of human habitation. European societies had a need for industrial revolution where Native Americans did not. Native Americans would never have found need for such endeavors since their societies were empowered by the land in which they dwelled. Native American cultures more than likely would have continued on their path of environmental harmony had they not encountered European peoples. First-nation people did not have philosophies or a religious basis that encouraged them to take more from the land than they needed. Wealth and status achieved through exploitation of the land was contrary to the fabric of their societies. It is out of thousands of years of stewardship that we examine the life of one Native American we know as Nancy Ward (Nan-ye-hi).[2]

Nan-ye-hi continued as an advocate for her country and nation for several years. She continued to speak of the necessity for her people to devote more attention to farming and raising stock as a means of survival. Nan-ye-hi's seeds were sown in fertile soil, and one of the last treaties with the Cherokee, Article 14 of the Holston River Treaty, guaranteed their ability and assistance in husbandry and agriculture as they continued to prosper in their land.

Another attempt at peace occurred in a meeting at Hopewell, North Carolina. This meeting was the first meeting of the United States Congress with any Native American nation. Congress disavowed all previous treaties promising the rights of the Cherokee to live on their land. Concessions were made to return parts of their territory then under control of white settlers. This agreement became known as the Hopewell Treaty. This treaty granted the Cherokee the right to remove any white settler from their homeland by force if necessary. The United States Congress never kept this agreement. Furthermore, they did not support the Cherokee when they began to remove settlers from their lands.

After the Hopewell Treaty failed miserably, other treaties were forthcoming. The treaties of 1817–1819 further eroded Cherokee homelands. United States commissioners resorted to bribery and other illegal means to obtain signers. The 2,000 who had already moved west were told they could have no western land until an equivalent acreage had been ceded in the east. This of course was a lie. As a result of this falsehood, fifteen western Cherokee chiefs were persuaded to sign by proxy. Well-placed bribes enticed thirty-one eastern chiefs to sign. The eastern chiefs who signed the cession papers moved west, fearful for their lives. By this time official Cherokee council leadership had passed a law that any chief that ceded additional land would be put to death. The transaction was bitterly resented by the Cherokee council and rejected by Cherokee national mandate.

Nan-ye-hi Ward addressed her nation for the last time on May 2, 1817:

> The Cherokee ladies now being present at the meetings of the chiefs and warriors in counsel have thought it their duty as mothers to address their beloved chiefs and warriors now assembled. … Nancy Ward to her children Warriors to take pity and listen to talks of your sisters, although I am very old yet cannot but pity the situation in which you will hear of their minds, I have great many grandchildren, which I wish them to do well on our land.[3]

This address was taken to the council meeting by Nan-ye-hi's son, Fivekiller, and accompanied by her distinctive walking cane, which represented her official vote and authority in her absence.

Nan-ye-hi might not have ever worshiped in a church. Scripture challenges us that authentic relationship is evident by visible fruit of the outward life we lead. Could it be there are many expressions of a life in Christ free from the label of savagery or paganism? Nan-ye-hi lived a Creator God-dominated life; she lived in a Creator God-dominated society. Subsequent to her life, her nation would not allow national office to be held by anyone who did not uphold these truths.

The unofficial Cherokee national anthem became "Amazing Grace."

Less than 5 percent of Native Americans profess a true relationship with Christ—they see Christianity as white man's religion. Many more than this, though, offer a yes to the response of being a Christian. This yes is tempered with generations of those who have been given the choice of being seen as "civilized" Christians or being killed. Most tribal people cannot find cultural identity within traditional Western Christendom. May God have mercy on those who have committed the genocide that has occurred under the banner of the cross.

Fire is important to the Cherokee. Women were keepers of the fire in their homes. Each year the women ceremoniously extinguished all flames within the tribe. One of the roles of the *Ghighau* was to reintroduce new fire.[4] In countless ceremonies, Nan-ye-hi would have helped in rekindling the fire within her tribe. It was said that if the principle people kept the fire burning, the Creator God would reveal truth. An eternal flame now burns at Red Clay, Tennessee. Red Clay was the last capital of a united tribe called the Cherokee prior to the Trail of Tears. God the Father wants us to spread truth to all people without the spin of our culture.

Reflect & Pray

1. Injustices permeate all nations and cultures. What is something you can do to help alleviate an injustice that you have witnessed?

2. What do you think about people who confess to love God but are not associated with a particular church or denomination? Is church membership necessary to be a follower of Christ Jesus?

3. What are a few ways Christians can reach out to the tribal nations?

4. How can you keep the fire of truth burning within your heart, home, and community?

Jesus, you are part of the tribe of Judah. You are a man of color, not a white man. You wore traditional regalia (special clothing). There was power associated with your clothing. (The woman who touched the hem of your garment.) You celebrated the many feasts of your Father. Your tribe's calendar is kept in cycles of the moon. Your Bible is a tribal book. You celebrated your ancestors (lineage of Christ). Your nation was led by tribal elders. Throughout your tribe's history, animals played important roles (whales, lions, bears, donkeys, ravens, doves). Your Bible celebrates the created order. (The trees will clap their hands.) You did nothing during your life of your own accord, but always stayed submitted to your Father's will. You used water as a sign of purification. You celebrated the land of your inheritance. You took nothing from it you did not need. Your nation fought fiercely all those who attempted to take your land from you. Your nation spared no one who lived within your enemy's camp. You upheld all your tribal laws. You upheld the strict religious practices of your tribe. Your Father held your nation accountable to past generations who did not keep their covenants. You are a Person who always keeps your word. You allowed false counsel to be spoken of you, without taking revenge, for the sake of your tribe. You died a tortured death at the hands of a conquering nation to save your people. All who come to you for their salvation are not saved apart from being in-grafted into your tribe.

Day 33

More Than a Nurse: Florence Nightingale (1820-1910)

> Study and do your best to present yourself to God approved,
> a workman [tested by trial] who has no reason to be ashamed,
> accurately handling and skillfully teaching the word of truth.
>
> 2 TIMOTHY 2:15

*F*lorence Nightingale was known as "the lady with the lamp," a nickname that was given to her by British soldiers who were wounded during the Crimean War in the mid-1850s.[1] They called her this because they always saw her carrying her lamp as she walked the halls of the hospital each night. Now this name has become a symbol of all that Florence stood for—a light of care for the sick, concern for soldiers' welfare, and freedom for women to choose what kind of work they want to do.

This founder of the modern nursing profession was not the romantic, gentle, retiring Victorian woman that some people might imagine. She was a bright, tough, driven professional who became a brilliant organizer and one of the most influential women of the 19th century.

When she was seventeen years old, God spoke to her heart at Embley, the family's winter home. She wrote, "On February 7, 1837, God spoke to me and called me into His service."[2] She felt strongly that He had given her a special mission in life. She suspected that this mission would involve helping others, something that Florence had always enjoyed doing. She studied, was eager, and certainly did her utmost to present herself to God as one who was approved. She had been tested by trial and had no reason to be ashamed. Through her marvelous example, we can learn so much because she showed us what it means to be a worker approved by God.

In March, 1853, Russia invaded Turkey. Britain and France were concerned about the rise of the Russian Empire so they responded to the invasion by declaring war on Russia in March, 1854. This was the beginning of the Crimean War.

Many soldiers had to endure great hardships as they fought in this bloody war. The death rate was very high due to wounds, typhus, cholera, malaria, and dysentery. Within a few weeks after the conflict began, 8,000 men were suffering from various diseases.

The London Times exposed the poor medical care that was being given to the British soldiers. This caused a public outcry for better medical care and Florence Nightingale responded to this need by offering her services. There was still considerable prejudice against women being involved in medicine in any capacity, so the British government officials rejected her offer at first. As time went on, however, they changed their minds because the need was so great.

Florence was given permission to take a group of 38 nurses to the military hospitals in Turkey. When she arrived at the Barak Hospital in the suburbs of Constantinople on November 4, 1854, Florence found the conditions totally appalling.

In the face of such seemingly insurmountable odds, many people would have despaired. Not Florence Nightingale; she persevered in her drive, compassion, and hard labor. She and her nurses scrubbed the wards. They washed the patients and dressed their wounds regularly, and they emptied the chamber pots daily.

Out of her own money Florence purchased 6,000 hospital gowns, 2,000 pairs of socks, and hundreds of nightcaps, slippers, plates, cups, and utensils. She hired 200 Turkish workers to restore the burned-out corridors, thus making room for an additional 800 patients.

In 1859, she published two books and raised funds to support her campaign to improve the quality of nursing. In 1860, when the Civil War was beginning in America, Florence founded the Nightingale School and Home for Nurses at St. Thomas's Hospital. She also became involved in the training of nurses for employment in workhouses.

This valiant woman addressed the subject of women's rights in her book, *Suggestions for Thought to Searchers after Religious Truths*. In this work, she argued for the removal of restrictions that prevented women from having careers.

Another book she wrote was titled *Suggestions for Thought to the Searchers after Truth among the Artizens of England*, which she kept revising until it seemed that God had spoken to her. He said, "You are here to carry out My program. I am not here to carry out yours." About this word from the Lord she wrote, "I must remember that God is not my private secretary!"

Florence Nightingale was passionate about what she knew God had called her to do and she moved in unfeigned compassion among the sick and dying. Her tireless efforts revolutionized medical care throughout the British Empire.

Florence went on to study new designs for modern hospitals all over Europe. In Paris she found a revolutionary design in which separate units or pavilions made up one large hospital, and each pavilion was a light and airy self-contained unit. This design helped to minimize infections among the patients.

Her expertise gained her a reputation in America and Britain. The United States asked for Florence's help in establishing military hospitals for soldiers in the Civil War and she was the first woman to receive the Order of Merit from the British government.

Due to overwork her health declined, and she spent the last half of her life frequently bedridden. When Florence was sixty-five years old, she wrote this on Christmas Day: "Today, O Lord, let me dedicate this crumbling old woman to thee; behold, the handmaid of the Lord. I was thy handmaid as a girl, since then I have backslid."

She died at the age of ninety and asked that the epitaph on her tombstone would read simply: "FN 1820 to 1910." She said that it would be a great honor for her to be buried in a casket that would be like those in which common soldiers are buried.[3]

Florence Nightingale was a lioness among women—one whose faith, strength, and courage allowed her to live a compassion-acts lifestyle wherever she went. We find a summation of her life and philosophy in something she wrote long ago:

> Life is a hard fight, a struggle, a wrestling with the Principle of Evil, hand-to-hand, foot-to-foot. Every inch of the way must be disputed. The night is given us to take breath, to pray, to drink deep at the fountain of power. The day, to use the strength which has been given to us, to go forth to work with it till the evening.

Reflect & Pray

1. Is there a certain profession that you have always thought or felt you would be good at? Is this the profession or career you are currently in? Why or why not?

2. Is there a certain profession at which you know you would not excel? Explain.

3. The compassion Florence felt for the wounded soldiers motivated her to seek improvements in their conditions. What moves you to action?

4. How can you lead a compassion-acts lifestyle? What are a few things you can do this week?

Dear heavenly Father, teach me to put you first in all that I do. Open my heart to serve the ones you put in my path. As I serve them, I serve you—my Redeemer and my Provider. May I look to you for guidance and not be satisfied with earthly wealth or status. My strength comes from you—may I use it to further your kingdom in my world. In Jesus' name, amen.

Approved by God:
Gladys Aylward (1902–1970)

I can do all things through Christ who strengthens me.

PHILIPPIANS 4:13 NKJV

When Gladys Aylward arrived in China as a missionary, three weeks after leaving London, exhausted and dirty, she was relieved the journey was complete but nervous about a long-awaited meeting with the formidable older missionary to whom she had been sent, Mrs. Lawson. Feeling unworthy and insignificant, much due to her unsightly appearance, she realized she had only one thing to offer—herself.

Mrs. Jeannie Lawson was from Scotland and rarely showed any sign of emotion. Rather harshly, Gladys was ushered into what was soon to be her new home. Gladys realized her hopes for a comfortable bed and warm bath were a bit premature when she walked into a partially-dilapidated house where a cement floor was her bed. When asked where she should change clothes, Mrs. Lawson politely told her to sleep in her clothes with all her belongings within hand's reach—having her things close made them harder to steal. Gladys began questioning her sanity for wanting to move to China. Apparently, the news of her arrival had spread around town and she awoke with dozens of faces peering into the open windows. At any rate, she was grateful for the advice of Mrs. Lawson to sleep in her clothes!

On weekends the duo would travel to villages, wait until crowds gathered to gaze in curiosity at the foreign ladies, and begin to preach the gospel. The villagers would stare in amazement as some had never before seen a white person, especially their feet. A Chinese custom required all women to have their feet bound, so Mrs. Lawson and Gladys' free feet always brought much attention.

Later on in the year, while Gladys was away from the inn, Mrs. Lawson had a terrible accident. She had fallen from the second-story balcony and had lain outside for over a week, exposed to the weather without any assistance from anyone. When Gladys returned, she found dear Mrs. Lawson lying on top of a pile of coal where she had fallen. Gladys cared for her and nursed her, but it became evident she was not going to recover. Shortly before she passed into heaven, Mrs. Lawson whispered to Gladys, "God called you to my side, Gladys, in answer to my prayers. He wants you to carry on my work here. He will provide. He will bless and protect you."[1]

Now being alone, Gladys kept the inn running and held gospel meetings in the evenings. She traveled around villages, caring for people and giving medical aid as best she could. Funds were extremely low. Mrs. Lawson had never told Gladys about a large yearly tax due to the mandarin, which Mrs. Lawson had paid out of her small monthly income. Now those funds were no longer available, and the payment was due. Unable to bear the thought of closing the inn and leaving China, she knew the only place to go was to the feet of her Jesus and offer the only thing she had to give—herself. The mandarin took her up on her offer and made her his official foot-binding inspector, assigned to travel to the remote villages to make sure that the young girls' feet were no longer being bound as had been customary.

As her understanding of the culture in this region grew, "Ai-weh-deh" (meaning Virtuous One, Gladys' Chinese name) became aware of the trade of buying and selling children. Her heart was continually being enlarged with every plight she discovered. How could she leave these little ones to suffer when she could do something on their behalf? One by one, she began adopting children. The first was Ninepence, followed by Less, Boa-Boa, Francis, and Lan Hsiang. Having adopted these children, she felt she needed to become a Chinese citizen so she would never be separated from them. The mandarin helped her fill out many papers, and in 1936 Gladys Aylward became the first foreign missionary to become a Chinese citizen.

The mandarin came to her regularly for help in solving problems. She started a school at the request of the prison governor. These were days of fulfillment and becoming really established in the region. However, there was a shadow of a problem in the distance that would soon knock on her door. War was about to envelope Yangcheng. Several years of conflict between Japan and China followed. During these years, regions went back and forth between Chinese and Japanese control.

Yangcheng was emptied on different occasions. The first time, under the counsel of Gladys, the prison governor, and the mandarin, everyone was told to leave the village and take their food and livestock, giving the Japanese no reason to stay. Gladys, because of her extensive travels throughout the region, knew a perfect hiding place—Bei Chai Chuang. It was ideal as there was no road that led to it, it was not on any map, and most importantly, the surrounding hills housed several large caves that were almost impossible to spot from the outside. This would become home to Gladys and her children for some time. Local people brought in food and supplies. A slow trickle of sick and wounded found their way to Gladys, knowing she would care for them. The cave was transformed into a hospital.

The war went on and on and the scorched-earth policy left many in need. The caves continued to be a place of safety; many came across the kindness and care of Gladys. When the number of children flooding in reached 150, Gladys stopped trying to keep count of them all. She endured many close calls with the Japanese. She ran through gunfire, wormed her way through wheat fields to escape, traveled along dangerous mountain trails hiding in clefts of rocks through the night, and endured the butt of a rifle on the side of her head, from which she never fully recovered.

"Flee, get you far off, dwell deep, O ye inhabitants of Hazor, saith the LORD; for Nebuchadrezzar king of Babylon hath taken counsel against you, and hath conceived a purpose against you" (Jeremiah 49:30 KJV). Her eyes read the verses from her Chinese Bible. Now she knew what she was to do! She gathered all the children together and put on every piece of clothing they had and tied around their waists every spare pair of shoes they could find. Their shoes were made of cloth and would barely last a day on the rugged trails they would climb. Everyone had to carry their own bedroll. The oldest children were around 15 years old, the youngest were barely four years of age. She wrapped all the food she had in a rag—barely enough millet for two days' rations—and she carried the old iron pot herself, to cook the millet in.

At every promise of being "almost there," there was always farther to go it seemed, more miles to walk, and the delays were many. Finally, after three weeks or more, they arrived at Fufeng, a city that was still receiving refugees.

On New Year's Day, 1970, Gladys simply did not wake up. She was 67 years old. Beside her bed was a newborn baby, sleeping peacefully. The baby had been abandoned and brought to Ai-weh-deh who received the baby with open, loving arms.

Reflect & Pray

1. Questioning your sanity when responding to God's call is not unusual. How have you handled times like these?

2. Have you ever been told that you were an answer to someone's prayers? Or have you told someone that he or she was the answer to *your* prayers? Pass along that good word to someone today and both of you will be blessed.

3. Gladys sheltered and protected the children. What is a way you can help children in your community?

4. How do you feel about the pro-life and pro-abortion controversy? Are there ways you can help the unborn in your community?

Father, I come to you in the name of Jesus. I pray that I would know your voice and your Word so well that I would be totally transformed by your Word and become a living epistle into the world where you are sending me. Oh Lord, may I be so in love with you that no obstacle would keep me from doing all I can do for your name's sake. May others' opinions not sway or affect my focus and determination to do all you have deposited in my heart. May I always remember that it is your approval and not others' that counts! In Jesus' name, amen.

Paragon of Compassion: Mother Teresa (1910–1997)

You have turned my mourning into dancing for me;
You have taken off my sackcloth and clothed me with joy.

PSALM 30:11

Mother Teresa of Calcutta (Agnes Gonxha Bojaxhiu) was born on August 27, 1910, in Skopje, which is in modern Macedonia. Her family was of Albanian descent, and she was the youngest of three children. At the age of twelve, Agnes strongly felt the call of God on her life, and she knew that she was destined to become a missionary. The overarching desire of her life from then on was to spread the love of Jesus Christ, particularly among the poor, the sick, and the outcasts of society.

When the Indian subcontinent was divided between India and Pakistan in 1947, a flood of over one million destitute refugees poured into Calcutta (now Kolkata). Most of these people were Hindus who had no concept of a personal God who was their heavenly Father. The majority of people who lived in Calcutta during the 1940s lived in the worst possible conditions of extreme hunger, deprivation, squalor, and filth.

Agnes, by then "Sister Teresa," gathered the city's throwaway children from rubbish heaps. Many were orphans. She explained, "We do our best to nurse them back to life."[1]

This valiant nun could see the life of Jesus in every child and adult and she approached each one as if he or she was the Lord Himself. She was their servant, an obedient follower of the One who said:

For I was hungry, and you gave Me something to eat; I was thirsty, and you gave Me *something* to drink; I was a stranger, and you invited Me in; *I was* naked, and you clothed Me; I was sick, and you visited Me [with help and ministering care]; I was in prison, and you came to Me [ignoring personal danger]. (Matthew 25:35–36)

Sister Teresa gave food to the hungry, hospitality to the strangers, clothes to the naked, and healing and practical help to the ill. She knew that in doing so she was ministering to the One who loves each person equally and without partiality.

In 1950 Sister Teresa was given permission by the Holy See to found a new order of Catholic nuns—the Missionaries of Charity. She was now Mother Teresa of Calcutta, the Mother Superior of this new order. She saw the order's primary task as being the provision of love and care for needy persons who had no one to help them.[2] Mother Teresa described their mission as follows:

[to care for] the hungry, the naked, the homeless, the crippled, the blind, the lepers, all those people who feel unwanted, unloved, uncared for throughout society, people that have become a burden to the society and are shunned by everyone.[3]

The Missionaries of Charity began with only twelve members in Calcutta. Today there are more than 4,000 nuns in the order throughout the world, and they minister to orphans, AIDS victims, refugees, the blind, the disabled, the aged, alcoholics, the poor, victims of natural disasters, and the hungry. The nuns can be found working in Asia, Africa, Latin America, North America, Poland, and Australia.

Mother Teresa always emphasized service to others. She believed and followed these words of Jesus: "And whosoever of you will be the chiefest, shall be servant of all" (Mark 10:44 KJV). She became a leader because she was a servant; she and her Sisters of Charity truly were the servants of all. Mother Teresa became known as "the saint of the gutter."

Pope John Paul II admired Mother Teresa, and he said that she was one of the greatest missionaries of the 20th century. He explained:

> The Lord made this simple woman who came from one of Europe's poorest regions a chosen instrument (cf. Acts 9:15) to proclaim the gospel to the entire world, not by preaching but by daily acts of love towards the poorest of the poor. A missionary with the most universal language: the language of love that knows no bounds or exclusion and has no preferences other than for the most forsaken. ... Where did Mother Teresa find the strength to place herself completely at the service of others? She found it in prayer and in the silent contemplation of Jesus Christ.[4]

I believe the pope was exactly right about the source of Mother Teresa's strength—prayer and the contemplation of her Lord and Master, Jesus Christ. This is the same place where you and I will find the strength we need to go forth in service as well; it is the secret place of the Most High.

She opened *Nirmal Hriday* ("Pure or Immaculate Heart"), a home for the dying, in 1952. This hospice became the focal point of her ministry for a couple of years. The government leaders of Calcutta gave her the use of a building for this purpose.

Writer Eileen Egan describes her work there as follows:

> I watched Mother Teresa as she sat on the parapet next to the low pallets of men, patting their heads or stroking their

stick-like arms, murmuring to each one. Sometimes only the eyes seemed alive in men whose skin was drawn so tightly that the skull seemed struggling to burst through. Some were even smiling, as though amazed to be alive. It was the same in the women's hall. Seeing me, they held out their wasted hands to me, searching for human consolation.

I turned away in fear and shame. I wondered how she could face day after day caring for those who were brought in covered with the filth and spittle of the gutter. Mother Teresa explained that her work and the work of the Sisters called for them to see Jesus in everyone, including the men and women dying in the gutter.[5]

Mother Teresa herself said these words:

Keep giving Jesus to your people not by words, but by your example, by your being in love with Jesus, by radiating His holiness and spreading His fragrance of love everywhere you go. Just keep the joy of Jesus as your strength. Be happy and at peace. Accept whatever He gives—and give whatever He takes with a big smile. You belong to Him.[6]

I love this simple statement of faith. Never forget that you are God's property, as Paul pointed out to the Corinthians: "You were bought with a price [you were actually purchased with the precious blood of Jesus and made His own]. So then, honor and glorify God with your body" (1 Corinthians 6:20).

Knowing that we are no longer our own, that we have been bought with a price, helps to clarify many things in our lives. It helps us to see what God wants us to do. It makes us realize that we do not have to do anything in our own strength. Surrender yourself to the One who created you and gave His life for you. Let Him live His life through you, as Mother Teresa did.

Through you, God can show people what David experienced: "You have turned my mourning into dancing for me; You have taken off my sackcloth and clothed me with joy" (Psalm 30:11).

Reflect & Pray

1. Mother Teresa was an example of living the language of love. What language do you live? How is God leading you to love those who are living in the slums of life?

2. Mother Teresa found strength in prayer and in the contemplation of her Lord. How has prayer and focusing on Jesus given you strength to do what God commands?

3. How can you spread the fragrance of Jesus to those you come in contact with each day?

4. What does it mean to you to belong to God?

Dear heavenly Father, in Jesus' name I come before you to offer my life to help your children—young and old—in whatever way is right and lovely in your eyes. May I follow the example of Jesus when He ministered to them out of love and compassion. Your example is the only example I need; your love is the only love I need to share with others—for it is pure and holy and nourishment to body and spirit. In the precious name of Jesus, amen.

Day 36

Five Empowered Women

> Now if any man build upon this foundation gold, silver,
> precious stones, wood, hay, stubble; every man's work shall be
> made manifest: for the day shall declare it, because it shall be
> revealed by fire; and the fire shall try every man's work
> of what sort it is. If any man's work abide …
>
> 1 CORINTHIANS 3:12–14 KJV

*G*od called each of these five ladies to acts of compassion and uncommon valor. They were women after God's own heart, ladies of character who lived their lives in sold-out commitment to the Father. As you read their stories, may you respond to His call as well, for He is looking for those who will obey Him by going forth into the whitened harvest fields during these last days of human history.

Amy Carmichael (1867–1951) founded the Dohnavur Fellowship for Girls in India, which was a ministry that was devoted to rescuing girls whose families had dedicated them to become temple prostitutes.

Through her ministry more than 1,000 children were rescued from abuse and neglect. The children called her "Amma," which means "mother" in the Tamil language, and Amy truly became a mother to them. She wrote:

> There were days when the sky turned black for me because of what I heard and knew was true. … Sometimes it was as if I saw the Lord Jesus Christ kneeling alone, as He knelt

long ago under the olive trees. … And the only thing that one who cared could do was to go softly and kneel down beside Him, so that He would not be alone in His sorrow over the little children.[1]

Amy Carmichael was a devout woman of prayer, and her life was characterized by total commitment, all-out compassion, obedience, and selflessness. Amy Carmichael wrote thirty-five books, many of which continue to inspire people around the world today. She was crippled by a fall in 1931, and four years later she became bedridden. She remained disabled thereafter and died in 1951, and was buried in her beloved Dohnavur.

For more than fifty years, Amy's overarching goal in life was:

To save children in moral danger; to train them to serve others; to succor the desolate and the suffering; to do anything that may be shown to be the will of our heavenly Father, in order to make His love known, especially to the people of India.[2]

Though she was rich, **Katharine Drexel** (1858–1955) voluntarily became a poor woman who ministered to the poor; she realized that everything she had belonged to God. "Mother Katharine" began to use her money for God. She started by building a convent in Bensalem, Pennsylvania, not far from her native Philadelphia. In her lifetime (1858–1955) she freely gave nearly twenty million dollars from her parents' estate to the poor. She established sixty missions to provide education for Native and African Americans, and she and her sisters dedicated their lives completely to the welfare of these disadvantaged people.[3]

Along the way, Mother Katharine and her sisters encountered

great opposition, particularly from people with racial prejudices. She never wavered in the face of conflict, however, and eventually won the respect of many people, even of former enemies. She always stood stalwartly for justice, mercy, and peace.

Katharine was a woman who believed in the power of prayer. She asked God to intervene in the lives of Native and African Americans and to stem the tide of racism in the United States. She recognized that these people were denied the rights of full citizenship and equality in many places and that those who were able to attend school received poor educations. As a result, she developed "a compassionate urgency to help change racial attitudes in the United States."[4]

In her lifetime of service to God and His Church she accomplished the founding of forty-nine convents for her sisters; the establishment of training courses for teachers; the building of sixty-two schools, including Xavier University; numerous writings; and helping to change the attitudes of church people toward the poor and disenfranchised.

Without any question, **Phoebe Palmer** (1807–1874) played a prominent role in spreading the concept of Christian holiness throughout America and around the world. She wrote several books on this topic including *The Way of Holiness,* a foundational book in the Holiness Movement. She was very influential in the lives of several women including Frances Willard, a leading advocate in the Temperance Movement, and Catherine Booth, the cofounder of the Salvation Army.

In her book, *The Promise of the Father,* Phoebe Palmer took a strong stand on behalf of the role of women in Christian ministry. Her teaching opened the door for many women preachers to respond to God's call on their lives.

Mrs. Palmer's holiness was reflected in every aspect of her life, and it impelled her to help found the Five Points Mission in a slum area of New York City in 1850. She also served as a leader in the Methodist Ladies' Home Missionary Society. Her faith had "legs" as it moved in compassion among the dregs of society.

Hannah More (1745–1833) was the most influential female member of the Society for Effecting the Abolition of the African Slave Trade in England and she counted William Wilberforce and John Newton (who wrote "Amazing Grace") among her friends. She wrote a number of religious tracts that eventually led to the formation of the Religious Tracts Society. Several of her tracts opposed slavery and the slave trade.

Clearly Hannah blazed a trail for women in her day. She believed in justice for all people. She was a pioneer in the abolitionist movement, which eventually brought an end to slavery in Great Britain and the United States. She chose to get involved in the world instead of living a life of quiet obscurity, which she could have chosen because she became quite wealthy as a result of the publication of her numerous books, plays, poems, and tracts.

Elizabeth Fry (1780–1845) and eleven other Quakers founded the Association for the Improvement of the Female Prisoners in Newgate Prison in London. In an address to the House of Commons, Elizabeth described the conditions of the women in Newgate Prison:

> each with a space of about six feet by two to herself … old and young, hardened offenders with those who had committed only a minor offence or their first crime; the lowest of women with the respectable married women and maid-servants.[5]

Her work influenced major changes in the penal system in Great Britain, which housed all sorts of criminals and punished them with tortures that were arbitrary at best. It was these unjust penalties and unfair conditions that caused Elizabeth Fry to get fully involved in prison reform. When she visited Newgate, she would often read the Bible to inmates.

Between 1818 and 1843, Elizabeth visited prisons throughout the British Isles and the continent of Europe. It was an exhausting and dangerous journey. She would seek the approval of local officials before entering the prisons, and after her visits she would organize a ladies' association to continue her work in each local prison.

These five women confronted the evils of their time. They acted out of the deep love and compassion of their Lord, seeking to help the suffering, the oppressed, the outcasts, and the needy. They became His hands and feet, devoting their lives to His call. Thousands of lives were touched because of their obedience—their willingness to give out of all that they had, relying on God to supply them with the courage and grace they would need.

Reflect & Pray

1. Of the five women featured today, with which one do you most closely identify? Why?
2. Of the five women featured, with which one do you identify the least? Why?
3. The individual talents, skills, and experiences of each of these five women vary greatly. How does this confirm that God uses the personal attributes of each of His children to further His kingdom?
4. List a few of your unique gifts that God could use to help change the world around you for the betterment of all.

Heavenly Father, help me to become a compassionate person. Have mercy upon me and change me from glory to glory, that your image might be perfected in me. I want to be like you, Father, and like your Son, the Lord Jesus Christ. Change my concepts, eradicate my prejudices, demolish my mental strongholds, transform my mind, and give me a strong desire to be merciful and compassionate to all I come in contact with. Let me be an agent of change in my world today. In Jesus' name, amen.

Day 37

Empowered Living:
Heidi Baker

> "The King will answer and say to them,
> I assure you *and* most solemnly say to you, to the extent
> that you did it for one of these brothers of Mine,
> *even* the least *of them*, you did it for Me."

MATTHEW 25:40

*T*enacity characterizes this petite blonde, who is originally from Laguna Beach, California. At the age of sixteen, when most Laguna teens lounged on the beach enjoying the party atmosphere of the era, Heidi was accepted as an American Field Service student. She was sent to a Choctaw Indian reservation in Mississippi where she was exposed to an environment of poverty that she had never seen before. It was here that she gave her life to Jesus and after a five-day fast, encountered the Lord in a dramatic way:

> On the night of the fifth day, I expectantly went to Roark's little Pentecostal church in the country and was drawn to the altar. I knelt down and lifted my arms to the Lord. Suddenly, I felt taken to a new heavenly place. Pastor Roark was preaching, but I couldn't hear his loud, powerful voice at all. God's glory came to me again, wrapping me in a pure and brilliant white light. I was overwhelmed by who He is. I had never felt so loved, and I began to weep. This time He spoke to me audibly. "I am calling you to be a minister and a missionary," He said. "You are to go to Africa, Asia, and England." Again my heart was pounding and racing. I thought I might die.

168

Then the Lord Jesus spoke to me and told me I would be married to Him. He kissed my hand, and it felt as if warm oil ran down my arm. I was overcome with love for Him. I knew at that moment that I would go anywhere anytime and say anything for Him. I was ruined for this world by His intense love and mercy in calling me to Himself.[2]

Full of the presence and love of Jesus, Heidi started telling everyone about Him—on the reservation and later in her high school. She talked the local Episcopal priest into letting her start a Christian coffeehouse in the parish hall and ministered every Friday night for several years—praying for the drug addicts, alcoholics, homeless, and demon-possessed people. In the meanwhile, she attended Southern California College (now Vanguard University).

During her last year in college in 1980, she met her husband, Rolland Baker, grandson of well-known missionaries to China, missionaries who had gained a place in the Church history books for their vital part in launching a revival among Chinese youth in the pre-Maoist years (see H.A. Baker's *Visions Beyond the Veil*). True to both Rolland's heritage and Heidi's calling, they discerned that they were called together to help bring revival among the poor. Their ministry would be incarnational. They would live like the people, learn the language and the culture from those on the street, suffer with them, and earn trust in the process. They married six months later and have since traveled as missionaries to Hong Kong, England, and Mozambique. Their work has extended from Africa into many other countries of the world:

The Lord had showed me thousands and thousands of children, and I believe we are called to care for millions of children. At first I was absolutely overwhelmed with that vision, and I thought, "God how could that ever happen?

How could we ever do that, just stopping for the one? I don't know how we could ever, ever do that." I was praying, crying, fasting and asking God, and He said that He would bring a great revival, and in this revival He would touch the hearts of pastors, and they would become fathers of the fatherless. He said that was His answer for these children. They would be literally cared for by these Mozambican pastors. And then He told me that the widows would cook for them and feed them, that the widows would help farm and that we were to build indigenous buildings made of mud and straw, buildings that fit in with every church. We would see these children cared for in families.[3]

Heidi and Rolland labored for years in Africa; this lifestyle eventually took a toll on Heidi's spirit. Her ever-expanding heart of love ached to do more:

Now in Africa we were seeing the sequel to the revival Rolland's grandfather saw among his orphans in China. That was not an isolated outpouring without further fruit. In it Rolland and I saw the heart of God. We saw how He feels about the lost and forgotten. We saw how He delights to use the helpless and hopeless to accomplish His best work. We saw His pleasure in revealing Himself to those humble and poor in spirit enough to appreciate Him. We saw His ability to use simple children to ignite revival. Now we are seeing Him do the same thing in Mozambique. And what He was doing in our children's center fired our appetites all the more for revival.[4]

Rather than burning out (physically and spiritually) on the mission field and giving up or being consumed with worry over funds and food shortages, rather than flickering out in middle age after decades of ministry, Heidi and Rolland are burning ever stronger, completely dependent on God. Heidi has come to know of the love of God more keenly through the suffering orphans they minister to daily—orphans who reflect the face and heart of God. Heidi wrote recently in her online ministry report:

It is a privilege beyond price to see the joy and affection of the Holy Spirit poured out like a waterfall on people who have known so much severe hardship, disappointment and bitter loneliness in their lives. ...

From the freezing cold gypsy huts of eastern Bulgaria to the 115-degree heat of Sudanese refugee camps, from the isolated native Inuits of arctic Canada to the dirt-poor subsistence farmers along the Zambezi River, we see ravenous desire for God among the poor and lowly. Jesus knows their suffering, and He will make it up to them. He will be their God, and they will be His people. He will use them to shame the wise and make the world jealous of their wealth toward Him.

... All I want to do is love God and care for His people. I find them in the garbage, under trees dying of AIDS. I'm just really simple. Jesus said, "Look into My eyes," and everything completely changed. His eyes are filled with love and passion and compassion. Jesus always stops for the dying man, the dying woman and the dying child. That's all I know, passion and compassion. He calls me to love every single person I see every single day.

Just focus on His face. You will only make it to the end if you can focus on His face. Focus on His beautiful face. You can't feed the poor, you can't go to the street, you can't see anything happen unless you see His face. One glance of His eyes, and we have all it takes to lie down. We're not afraid to die.[5]

Reflect & Pray

1. Many extol the benefits of fasting. How has God used periods of fasting to speak more directly to you?

2. Have you ever been exposed to an environment of extreme poverty? What was your reaction?

3. Find on the map: Mozambique, Bulgaria, arctic Canada, and China. Pray for these countries and the people who have never heard the name of Jesus. Consider choosing a country and praying regularly for the people there.

4. Sometimes the neediest people a missionary can reach are right in their own neighborhoods. Think of an area of your town or city that is in need of God's truth and light. Are there ways you can forge a path into this area? Pray about it; then take action.

Dear Lord God Almighty, thank you for the strength and courage you have given those who are laid-down lovers of you. Thank you for those who reach out to the poor—one child, one person at a time. Help me to become like those who seek to help and comfort. I need your face before me to focus on and to draw power from—I need you to show me the way. In the precious name of Jesus, amen.

Day 38

Make It Personal

> But you, beloved, building yourselves up on
> your most holy faith, praying in the Holy Spirit, keep
> yourselves in the love of God, looking for the mercy of
> our Lord Jesus Christ unto eternal life. And on some have
> compassion, making a distinction.

JUDE 20–22 NKJV

There are many champions—both great and small—who have made it into "God's Hall of Heroes." Some of these good people we may never meet nor know until we see them in heaven, but others such as Rolland and Heidi Baker of Iris Ministries, are modern-day trailblazers and pacesetters from whom each of us can learn a great deal.

All too often we focus on the gigantic exploits that are done by great people of faith, but we must never forget that little acts of love and kindness often precede public displays of power. Each of us must go through a hidden preparation period in which we learn how to walk in compassion, and as in any process we have to take "baby steps" at first. This is the seed-planting stage.

Michal Ann and I had the pleasure of knowing Mahesh and Bonnie Chavda for many years. As many already know, it was the healing prayers of Mahesh Chavda which paved the way for the Lord to bless us with our four beautiful children. I have often said, "Mahesh is not a show horse; he is a work horse!"

In the earlier days of my ministry, I had the privilege of doing some behind-the-scenes work for Mahesh's meetings as he traveled around the United States and internationally. I remember getting drinks for him, serving as a "catcher," fetching his tennis shoes so his tired feet could be more comfortable after praying with people until 2 a.m., and enjoying the fun of non-religious fellowship with him.

What always impressed me the most as I observed and learned from Mahesh was how he always took time for each individual. He never seemed to be in a rush; he ministered to each person as though every single individual was the most important person in the meetings. The Bakers and the Chavdas are both great, modern-day examples of the power of taking time for the one—always making it personal. The following is a story that was taken from Mahesh's first book, *Only Love Can Make a Miracle*. It shows how his heart of compassion and his ministry began to bloom:

The Lord gave me an overwhelming love for children. It was hard to explain. It was as though the Lord broke off a little piece of His heart and placed it inside me. I loved those children as though they were my own.

I used to work a nine-hour shift in Lily, usually with the ambulatory children, those who were able to get around on their own. When I was off duty, I would go to the non-ambulatory wards just to be with the children there. I had such a love for them. The thought of them having to spend the rest of their lives in those cribs almost broke my heart.

I knew that God loved them, too, and that He wanted to channel that love through me. I didn't really know what to do with them or even how to pray for them. I used to just hold them and pray quietly in the Spirit. Often I would sit in a rocking chair with one of them for hours, just praying and singing in tongues.

One little girl especially touched my heart. Her name was Laura. Laura's mother had been using hard drugs during pregnancy, and she had been born blind and severely retarded. I used to rotate through the different non-ambulatory wards on my after-hours visits, but in time I began to gravitate more and more to little Laura. She was so precious to me.

One day I had occasion to go into Laura's ward during the day. It had been several weeks since I had started holding her and praying with her. As I approached her crib, she turned toward me and stretched out her hands to welcome me! There were a number of staff members nearby. They were amazed. They kept saying to each other, "Did you see that?" Laura had never shown any outward response to anyone before, not even to being touched. Now she was responding to me from across the room. Could it be that she was gaining her sight? Could it be that the Lord was healing her through my prayers?

Not long after this, I had a similar experience with a little boy who had been born with a terrible birth defect. His spine was deformed so that he was unable to sit up. Again, after I had been praying with him over a period of several weeks, he suddenly became able to sit up. His back was healed!

As far as I can recall, I never once specifically prayed that these children be healed. I had prayed that way for my mother because I felt the Lord had told me to. Other than that, prayer for healing was not something I was accustomed to doing.

When I was with the children, I would simply hold them and pray that the Lord would somehow enable them to experience His love through me. I was as surprised as anyone when they started getting better.

I was learning many lessons in my school of the Spirit. Now I was learning that the power of God was to be found in the love of God. When the Lord sent me to the State School, he did not say, "I am sending you as My ambassador of power or of miracles." He said, "I am sending you as My ambassador of love." That was the way I saw myself and that was the way I prayed for the children: that the Lord would make His love real to them. The healings came almost as a by-product. I learned that only love can make a miracle.[2]

Will you be an ambassador of love for the Father? His love is powerful; it truly is the stuff of which miracles are made.

First, we have to perceive the need. Then, we speak words of encouragement and comfort which may often lead us to communicate love and warmth through a touch or an embrace. Next, we take action by doing what we can to provide practical help and assistance to the person in need. One thing we can always do is to pray for him or her, and, as Tennyson said, "More things are wrought by prayer than this world dreams of."

Deep within His spirit, Jesus is always in tune with the Father. His intimacy with His Father propelled Him to go out among the people and to be sensitive to their needs. In other words, He looked outside Himself and He saw what others needed. We can do the same, but first we must spend time alone with God in the secret place of the Most High. That is time well spent, for it empowers us to go forth in love and compassion.

A deep yearning arises as we spend time with the Father, and this yearning is focused on helping others.

Reflect & Pray

1. Reflect on a few "little acts of love and kindness" you can you perform today and for whom. Then take action.

2. What does it mean to be an ambassador of love for the Father?

3. "Only love can make a miracle." Reflect about why this phrase is true.

4. Take fifteen minutes to spent time alone with God in the secret place of the Most High today, seeking His face and listening to His voice.

Jesus, be big in me! Let your emotions within me be stirred up. By your grace, I choose to sow seeds of your radical transforming love and mercy into the lives of others. I volunteer freely to be a part of your compassionate army walking throughout the nations to bring a revival of kindness. I want to make a difference! Here I am—use me! Amen and amen!

Empowerment through Compassion

Thus has the Lord of hosts said, "Dispense true justice and practice kindness and compassion, to each other; and do not oppress or exploit the widow or the fatherless, the stranger or the poor; and do not devise or even imagine evil in your hearts against one another."

ZECHARIAH 7:9–10

We have journeyed through the Scriptures, studying God's heart for justice, righteousness, and mercy. We have looked up close and personal at the lives of some amazing women and their impact on the world. Now, it's time to really get personal. Before we go any further though, we are going to rest. Rest is a very important key, especially in regard to this call to compassion. As we open our hearts to feel God's heart, we may feel pressure to "do" something. Where is this pressure coming from? Is it direction from God, or are we beginning to see legitimate needs but moving out of our mental or soulish strength rather than out of our spirit? Ah, this is very important! Take time right now to stop and rest. Let your mind and heart center on His presence and worship Him for just a few minutes.

Compassion ministry, or whatever you want to call it, can be very draining and exhausting. But it doesn't have to be. It depends on your motivation and your approach. It should not drive you, but rather God's heart should lead you. Do you see the difference?

Do you remember the story about Mary and Martha? In the

past, I heard that "Mary chose the better part," and that Martha was reprimanded.

We need to look at the Scripture again. Part of the story takes place in John 11, and it revolves around Lazarus, who was Mary and Martha's brother. Mary was the one who had anointed Jesus' feet with perfume and wiped His feet with her hair. She was also the one who just wanted to sit at His feet and listen to Him speak, while Martha was in the kitchen preparing food (see Luke 10:38–39). There has been a lot of emphasis on Mary in recent years and the place in God she typifies. We all need to have the heart of Mary— loving to sit at His feet, period.

Martha, dear Martha! She was the one who received Jesus and welcomed Him into her house. Now, she did become distracted with much serving, and that was the point that Jesus spoke tenderly to her, redirecting her heart to "the better part," to worship Him (see Luke 10:41–42). But I believe He was wooing her, drawing her to Himself, not correcting or belittling her. She had messed up, had an attitude problem, and had compared her serving and cooking to Mary's sitting. What a common error that is—a lesson we are still trying to learn.

When Lazarus was sick, the sisters sent word to Jesus (see John 11). Although Jesus loved Lazarus, He did not come right away, but rather waited until Lazarus died. By the time He came, Lazarus had been in the tomb for four days. John wrote:

> So when Martha heard that Jesus was coming, she went to meet Him, while Mary remained sitting in the house. Then Martha said to Jesus, "Lord, if You had been here, my brother would not have died. Even now I know that whatever You ask of God, God will give to You." (John 11:20–22)

Do you see a pattern? Not only was it Martha who welcomed Jesus into her house, and in that, to her city, but when her brother died, she was the one who met Him, and asked for her brother's life to be restored. We need Martha! It doesn't have to be, "Are you a Mary or a Martha?" The point? God wants us to be both. There is no place for comparison in the kingdom of God, and we don't have to choose between either living a life of prayer and devotion or serving—we are to choose both! If in the past, you've considered yourself a Mary or a Martha and making that determination has disqualified you from being in the other camp, the wall is now torn down and the camp enlarged. It's time for Mary and Martha to come together. After all, they were sisters, and they did live in the same house. So should we!

I've had a thought come to me concerning all this. Once when I was in a deep place in prayer on the hard stone floor of the Elijah Inn in Pemba, Mozambique, I believe the Lord showed me something. As I lay there, while deep in a place of travail, intense heat, and all of our team groaning and laboring for God's justice to be established in the land, I saw the body of Christ. I saw the call to have compassion and to act. But then I saw something else. The body thought it was functioning well and performing the will of God, but in actuality it had no bowel! It did not even realize that it was missing a major body part—one of the most important organs where most of the nutrition comes from and feeds and brings nourishment to all the other body parts.

Of course, we need to pray—really pray that we get this, both individually and corporately. We need to pray for a miraculous release! The Lord has been showing different people that there are rooms in heaven that are full of body parts waiting for a wave of unprecedented healing anointing to be released. Why not pray for supernatural release for the body—a wave of unprecedented compassion across all lands, to all people groups, tribes, tongues, and nations?

The world is literally screaming at us, desperate for help. According to recent studies, 75 percent of the world's population lives in poverty. Most of these people live in third world or developing countries. The average annual gross income for individual workers in Western countries is $27,000. Contrast that with the rest of the world, where the average annual gross income is between $450 and $2,500 per person.[1] What a difference!

Approximately 50 percent of the world's population is female. Women and girls suffer more from poverty than men. Forty percent of the world's population consists of children. They are the ones who suffer more than all others. In fact, over one billion children are at risk today, and many have become actual victims of extreme poverty, homelessness, the loss of their parents, child labor, abuse, slavery, sexual exploitation, AIDS and other illnesses, and the effects of war and religious persecution.[2]

In certain parts of the world, orphaned children are conscripted into armies and suffer sexual, mental, and physical abuse. They are forced to carry guns and trained to kill. At times, the governments involved are willing to "sell off" numbers of these children to ease their financial situations. Finances are needed today for these purposes. I know of dear, precious saints who are working behind the lines to rescue these children and give them hope for their destiny and restore self-respect and self-esteem.

If those children were our children, or those people our family, don't you think our attitude would be different? I know mine would! And yet, that is what the Lord wants to do—enlarge our hearts to such a degree that "they" become "our family." They are His kids, the love of His heart, and we just don't seem to get it or care. When will we get it? When will we engage and do something about these needs?

Reflect & Pray

1. With whom do you more quickly identify—Mary or Martha? Why? How are both Marys and Marthas important in God's grand plan?

2. Do you know Marys and Marthas who have learned to work together to His glory? How can you adapt your natural abilities to complement others who are advancing His kingdom?

3. Children are so vulnerable. What steps can you take to help the least of these in your church, community, state, nation, and world?

4. Read a magazine, newspaper, or Internet article about the plight of women and children worldwide. Ask God how He wants you to make a difference.

Father of all, thank you for the love and compassion you show me each and every day. Thank you for your faith and mercy, your grace and power, and your Son Jesus Christ in whom I trust and believe with all my heart. May your goodness be spread throughout the world. In the precious name of Jesus, amen.

Day 40

Become Empowered Today

You are the [awesome] God who works [powerful] wonders;
You have demonstrated Your power among the people.

PSALM 77:14

*W*e need to ask for answers to questions the world has yet to ask. We need to look into the future and ask the Lord for creative solutions and inventions. We need to look at ways to create entrepreneurial businesses to create jobs for those in low-income areas and help boost economies. We need to ask for houses and look for ones that can be salvaged, repaired, and used for places of recovery or rescue.

How about a marriage of compassion with the prophetic? How about building relationships with our police, finding out the needs of our cities, and developing prophetic intercessory teams who will pray and ask for specific answers? We need to see what we can do to rescue and create a net to catch the women and children who have been trapped in sex trade businesses and prostitution and are looking for a way out.

We need to develop water filtration systems that are inexpensive and easy to set up and establish in third world countries, and we need to develop supply lines so ministries learn to work together and serve each other. We need to bring help in such a way that it releases blessing to whole areas. We need to cross over boundary lines of denominations and affiliations, reaching into areas that just plain need help. We need to move forward in kingdom understandings and applications and build relationally and, most importantly, in love.

We need to care for the poor and needy, the widow and orphan, not only within our own regions, but we need to have an international expression as well. Africa is dying right now! Our help is needed right now. They need simple things—beans and rice—by the trailer loads. Whole families are being lost. Here in the United States, most major cities are full of kids who have run away from home; they are living on the streets and taking drugs. These are our kids—these are our people. Jesus, open our eyes and hearts!

Being raised in rural Missouri from birth until James and I were married, I have a great appreciation for the figurative language regarding nature and agriculture that is used in the Bible. I spent many, many hours in the hot sun with an ever-aching back and sunburned arms weeding our huge vegetable garden, harvesting those vegetables, and preparing and storing them. We kept the kitchen stove running for days at a time canning beans, tomatoes, and various fruits. We processed countless chickens, cutting them up and freezing them. We processed cherries, peaches, apples, pears, raspberries, and plums.

We spent whole days at my grandmother's house fighting our way through endless blackberry thickets, actually creating tunnels through the tangled maze of thorny canes, and coming home with tubs and tubs full to put in the freezer. I've worked out in the hayfields with my brothers, running the tractor so they could pick up the bales and stack them on the wagon. That hay was necessary for our cattle to make it through the winter. I've known the necessity and value of tending plants, gardens, and fields:

Now when you reap the harvest of your land, you shall not reap to the very corners of your field, nor shall you gather the gleanings (grain left after reaping) of your harvest. And you shall not glean your vineyard, nor shall you gather its fallen grapes; you shall leave them for the poor and for the stranger. I am the Lord your God. (Lev. 19:9–10)

I believe the Lord is issuing a challenge to us, for we all have "fields" that we are laboring in—fields the Lord has given to us. It's in these fields that we must plant the seeds that will bring forth a bountiful harvest. Everyone has a sphere of influence—it may be your workplace, it may be your home, it may be the school you attend, it may be your ethnic background or the region where you live.

We must prepare our fields in such a way that we allow the poor and the strangers to benefit from the harvest. The times in which we live make this a very urgent matter, for we see a great increase in natural disasters, terrorism, war, and disease around the globe.

Plant good seed in your field and be sure to plant what God tells you to plant. While you do so, make certain that you leave some fruit in your field so that the poor can reap some from your harvest too.

The seventh year was meant to be a year of rest and rejoicing. The Bible says:

But the seventh year you shall let it rest and lie uncultivated, so that the poor among your people may eat [what the land grows naturally]; whatever they leave the animals of the field may eat. You shall do the same with your vineyard and olive grove. (Exodus 23:11)

As we get to know the heart of God, we need to get our lives in line with His calendar. The seventh year represents perfection and completion, a fulfillment of the will of God, which demands that the land should lie fallow so the poor can reap a benefit and so the land can rest.

The seventh year was a year of breakthrough and blessing both for the landowners and the poor. Everyone shared in the good things God had provided for them. In the Book of Esther we read:

> Because on those days the Jews rid themselves of their enemies, and as the month which was turned for them from grief to joy and from mourning into a holiday; that they should make them days of feasting and rejoicing and sending choice portions *of food* to one another and gifts to the poor. (Esther. 9:22, emphasis by the authors).

We need to enlarge our hearts to include the poor as part of our times of celebration. When deliverance, in whatever form it may take, comes to your house, remember as you enter into celebration that God's heart is for you to remember the poor. Let your deliverance spill over to those who are still waiting for their own deliverance to be released.

We have looked at compassion and the heart of God from many different angles. We have now come to the culmination of these many pages. Now is the moment of decision. Time is an intriguing element. We have a past and we speak of a future. But where both become a reality is right now. In reality, now is all that we have. We can do nothing about our past, but if we act now, we can establish what will become our past. We can talk about the future, but the problem is the future is always ahead of us—we can never live in the future.

We must live in the *now*. If we try to live in the future, we're always dreaming and never realizing. We need to take our dreams and make practical steps today to see them come to pass. We need to move out of any remorse over past mistakes or missed opportunities and make a decision to get up and act now!

Taking action means accepting the power God gives you to work His righteousness in the world. Become empowered today … and each day that you obey His perfect plan for your life.

Reflect & Pray

1. How can you become empowered by empowering others?

2. What are stumbling blocks that have kept you from taking action to reach out to others? Allowing God to empower you will cause you to step easily over those blocks.

3. What does the "seventh year" mean to you? How can you make this year one you look back on with joy.

4. What will you do *now* to fulfill your God-given destiny, knowing that He has empowered you to accomplish all that He designed especially for you to lead an abundant and victorious life?

Dear Lord Jesus, I come to you this day, volunteering myself to be your arms, your feet, your hands to hurting and needy people. I want to embrace your heart for the poor, the orphan and the widow. I want to offer to you the field you have given me, that you would show me how to help provide for those who are less fortunate. Lord, I ask you to speak to me, lead me into the avenues of service that I am to engage in. Lord, according to James 1:5, give me the wisdom I need to move forward; connect me with the people I need to network with. Today I make a commitment in my heart, with my mouth, to show you and the world my faith, by my works—because I love you, and I know that you so love me! In Jesus' name, amen!

Courage and
Strength
in God's Word

Confidence

Then the LORD turned to him and said, "Go with the strength you have, and rescue Israel from the Midianites. I am sending you!"

(Judges 6:14 NLT)

[The righteous] are confident and fearless
and can face their foes triumphantly.

(Psalm 112:9 NLT)

Therefore, brothers and sisters, since we have confidence to enter the Most Holy Place by the blood of Jesus, by a new and living way opened for us through the curtain, that is, his body, and since we have a great priest over the house of God, let us draw near to God with a sincere heart and with the full assurance that faith brings, having our hearts sprinkled to cleanse us from a guilty conscience and having our bodies washed with pure water.

(Hebrews 10:19–22 NIV)

Compassion

But you, Lord, are a compassionate and gracious God,
  slow to anger, abounding in love and faithfulness.

(Psalm 86:15 NIV)

"Show mercy and compassion for others, just as your
heavenly Father overflows with mercy and compassion
for all."

(Luke 6:36 TPT)

Indeed we count them blessed who endure. You have
heard of the perseverance of Job and seen the end *intended
by* the Lord—that the Lord is very compassionate and
merciful.

(James 5:11 NKJV)

The Lord is good to all;
  he has compassion on all he has made.

(Psalm 145:9 NIV)

Courage

Be strong and of good courage, for to this people you shall divide as an inheritance the land which I swore to their fathers to give them.

(Joshua 1:6 NKJV)

So don't lose your bold, courageous faith, for you are destined for a great reward!

(Hebrews 10:35 TPT)

Then David said to Solomon his son, "Be strong and courageous and do it. Do not be afraid and do not be dismayed, for the LORD God, even my God, is with you. He will not leave you or forsake you, until all the work for the service of the house of the LORD is finished.

(1 Chronicles 28:20 ESV)

"Look! He has placed the land in front of you. Go and occupy it as the LORD, the God of your ancestors, has promised you. Don't be afraid! Don't be discouraged!"

(Deuteronomy 1:21 NLT)

Freedom

Yet, Christ paid the full price to set us free from the curse of the law. He absorbed it completely as he became a curse in our place.

(Galatians 3:13 TPT)

For when we died with Christ we were set free from the power of sin.

(Romans 6:7 NLT)

Now the Lord is the Spirit, and where the Spirit of the Lord is, there is freedom.

(2 Corinthians 3:17 NIV)

"Everyone who believes in him is set free from sin and guilt—something the law of Moses had no power to do."

(Acts 13:39 TPT)

Hope

But the needy will not be ignored forever;
    the hopes of the poor will not always be crushed.

(Psalm 9:18 NLT)

As for me, I will always have hope;
    I will praise you more and more.

(Psalm 71:14 NIV)

Not only that, but we rejoice in our sufferings, knowing
that suffering produces endurance, and endurance
produces character, and character produces hope, and
hope does not put us to shame, because God's love has
been poured into our hearts through the Holy Spirit who
has been given to us.

(Romans 5:3–5 ESV)

Grace

Gracious is the LORD, and righteous;
Yes, our God is merciful.

(Psalm 116:5 NKJV)

Sin is no longer your master, for you no longer live under the requirements of the law. Instead, you live under the freedom of God's grace.

(Romans 6:14 NLT)

For the grace of God has appeared that offers salvation to all people.

(Titus 2:11 NIV)

Each time he said, "My grace is all you need. My power works best in weakness." So now I am glad to boast about my weaknesses, so that the power of Christ can work through me.

(2 Corinthians 12:9 NLT)

Guidance

I will bless the LORD who guides me;
  even at night my heart instructs me.

(Psalm 16:7 NLT)

The LORD is my revelation-light to guide me along the way;
  he's the source of my salvation to defend me every day.

(Psalm 27:1 TPT)

He teaches my hands to make war,
So that my arms can bend a bow of bronze.

(2 Samuel 22:35 NKJV)

Whether you turn to the right or to the left, your ears will
hear a voice behind you, saying, "This is the way; walk in it."

(Isaiah 30:21 NIV)

Intimacy

Remain in me, as I also remain in you. No branch can bear fruit by itself; it must remain in the vine. Neither can you bear fruit unless you remain in me.

(John 15:4 NIV)

I want to know Christ and experience the mighty power that raised him from the dead. I want to suffer with him, sharing in his death, so that one way or another I will experience the resurrection from the dead!

(Philippians 3:10–11 NLT)

And you must love the LORD your God with all your heart, all your soul, and all your strength.

(Deuteronomy 6:5 NLT)

Draw near to God and He will draw near to you. Cleanse your hands, you sinners; and purify your hearts, you double-minded.

(James 4:8 NKJV)

Justice

For the righteous LORD loves justice.
  The virtuous will see his face.

(Psalm 11:7 NLT)

You're a God who makes things right,
  giving justice to the defenseless.

(Psalm 103:6 TPT)

"Rejoice, O Gentiles, with His people;
For He will avenge the blood of His servants,
And render vengeance to His adversaries;
He will provide atonement for His land and His people."

(Deuteronomy 32:43 NKJV)

"For I, the LORD, love justice.
  I hate robbery and wrongdoing.
I will faithfully reward my people for their suffering
  and make an everlasting covenant with them."

(Isaiah 61:8 NLT)

Leadership

And the LORD commissioned Joshua the son of Nun and said, "Be strong and courageous, for you shall bring the people of Israel into the land that I swore to give them. I will be with you."

(Deuteronomy 31:23 ESV)

The LORD told Joshua, "Today I will begin to make you a great leader in the eyes of all the Israelites. They will know that I am with you, just as I was with Moses."

(Joshua 3:7 NLT)

Then all the tribes of Israel went to David at Hebron and told him, "We are your own flesh and blood. In the past, when Saul was our king, you were the one who really led the forces of Israel. And the LORD told you, 'You will be the shepherd of my people Israel. You will be Israel's leader.' "

(2 Samuel 5:1–2 NLT)

"But commission Joshua, and encourage and strengthen him, for he will lead this people across and will cause them to inherit the land that you will see."

(Deuteronomy 3:28 NIV)

Perseverance

But the one who looks into the perfect law, the law of liberty, and perseveres, being no hearer who forgets but a doer who acts, he will be blessed in his doing.

(James 1:25 ESV)

Do not be afraid of what you are about to suffer. I tell you, the devil will put some of you in prison to test you, and you will suffer persecution for ten days. Be faithful, even to the point of death, and I will give you life as your victor's crown.

(Revelation 2:10 NIV)

"Because you have obeyed my command to persevere, I will protect you from the great time of testing that will come upon the whole world to test those who belong to this world."

(Revelation 3:10 NLT)

For we are mingled with the Messiah, if we will continue unshaken in this confident assurance from the beginning until the end.

(Hebrews 3:14 TPT)

Power

For God will never give you the spirit of fear, but the Holy Spirit who gives you mighty power, love, and self-control.

(2 Timothy 1:7 TPT)

His divine power has given us everything we need for a godly life through our knowledge of him who called us by his own glory and goodness.

(2 Peter 1:3 NIV)

Although he was crucified in weakness, he now lives by the power of God. We, too, are weak, just as Christ was, but when we deal with you we will be alive with him and will have God's power.

(2 Corinthians 13:4 NLT)

I also pray that you will understand the incredible greatness of God's power for us who believe him. This is the same mighty power that raised Christ from the dead and seated him in the place of honor at God's right hand in the heavenly realms.

(Ephesians 1:19–20 NLT)

Provision

Then God said, "Look! I have given you every seed-bearing plant throughout the earth and all the fruit trees for your food. And I have given every green plant as food for all the wild animals, the birds in the sky, and the small animals that scurry along the ground—everything that has life." And that is what happened.

(Genesis 1:29–30 NLT)

"Everything in Israel that is devoted to the LORD is yours."

(Numbers 18:14 NIV)

Thus the LORD gave to Israel all the land that he swore to give to their fathers. And they took possession of it, and they settled there.

(Joshua 21:43 ESV)

LORD, you alone are my portion and my cup;
    you make my lot secure.
The boundary lines have fallen for me in pleasant places;
    surely I have a delightful inheritance.

(Psalm 16:5–6 NIV)

Purpose

His destiny-plan for the earth stands sure.
    His forever-plan remains in place and will never fail.

(Psalm 33:11 TPT)

The LORD works everything together to accomplish
        his purpose.
    Even the wicked are included in his plans—
he sets them aside for the day of disaster.

(Proverbs 16:4 TPT)

So we are convinced that every detail of our lives is continually woven together to fit into God's perfect plan of bringing good into our lives, for we are his lovers who have been called to fulfill his designed purpose.

(Romans 8:28 TPT)

The LORD will perfect that which concerns me;
Your mercy, O LORD, endures forever;
Do not forsake the works of Your hands.

(Psalm 138:8 NKJV)

Security

You need not be afraid of sudden disaster
  or the destruction that comes upon the wicked,
for the Lord is your security.
  He will keep your foot from being caught in a trap.
(Proverbs 3:25–26 TPT)

We know that God's children do not make a practice of
sinning, for God's Son holds them securely, and the evil
one cannot touch them.
(1 John 5:18 NLT)

Though many wish to fight and the tide of battle turns
    against me,
  by your power I will be safe and secure;
  peace will be my portion.
(Psalm 55:18 TPT)

The righteous will never be removed,
  but the wicked will not dwell in the land.
(Proverbs 10:30 ESV)

Trust

All you who fear the LORD, trust the LORD!
   He is your helper and your shield.

(Psalm 115:11 NLT)

Trust in the LORD forever,
   for the LORD God is an everlasting rock.

(Isaiah 26:4 ESV)

To all the rich of this world, I command you not to be wrapped in thoughts of pride over your prosperity, or rely on your wealth, for your riches are unreliable and nothing compared to the living God. Trust instead in the one who has lavished upon us all good things, fulfilling our every need.

(1 Timothy 6:17 TPT)

But the LORD said to Moses and Aaron, "Because you did not trust me enough to demonstrate my holiness to the people of Israel, you will not lead them into the land I am giving them!"

(Numbers 20:12 NLT)

Victory

After the death of Joshua, the Israelites asked the Lord, "Which tribe should go first to attack the Canaanites?" The Lord answered, "Judah, for I have given them victory over the land."

(Judges 1:1–2 NLT)

I wait quietly before God,
   for my victory comes from him.

(Psalm 62:1 NLT)

The sting of death is sin, and the power of sin is the law. But thanks be to God! He gives us the victory through our Lord Jesus Christ.

(1 Corinthians 15:56–57 NIV)

Your hand will be lifted up in triumph over your enemies,
   and all your foes will be destroyed.

(Micah 5:9 NIV)

Wisdom

If any of you lacks wisdom, you should ask God, who gives generously to all without finding fault, and it will be given to you.

(James 1:5 NIV)

Fear of the LORD teaches wisdom;
  humility precedes honor.

(Proverbs 15:33 NLT)

With God are wisdom and might;
  he has counsel and understanding.
If he tears down, none can rebuild;
  if he shuts a man in, none can open.

(Job 12:13–14 ESV)

How then does a man gain the essence of wisdom?
  We cross the threshold of true knowledge
  when we live in obedient devotion to God.
  Stubborn know-it-alls will never stop to do this,
  for they scorn true wisdom and knowledge.

(Proverbs 1:7 TPT)

Notes

Day 4 *Courage for the Cause: Joan of Arc*

1. Herbert Thurston, *The Catholic Encyclopedia* (New York, NY: Robert Appleton Company, 1996), s.v. "St. Joan of Arc," http://www.newadvent.org/cathen/08409c.htm.

2. Francis W. Leary, *The Golden Longing* (New York: Scribner, 1959), 44.

3. Thurston.

Day 5 *Faithful unto Death: Vibia Perpetua*

1. Catholic Online, "Sts. Perpetua and Felicity," Catholic.org, http://www.catholic.org/saints/saint.php?saint_id=48.

2. Peter Dronke, *Women Writers of the Middle Ages* (New York, NY: Cambridge University Press, 1984), 1–4.

3. Alban Butler, "St. Perpetua, and Felicitas, mm. with their Companions," *The Lives of the Fathers, Martyrs and Other Principal Saints.*

Day 6 *I Met God: Sojourner Truth*

1. Arthur H. Fauset, *Sojourner Truth, God's Faithful Pilgrim* (New York, NY: Russell & Russell, 1971), 57–63.

2. Harriet B. Stowe, "Sojourner Truth, The Libyan Sibyl," *Atlantic Monthly*, April 1863, 473–481, http://etext.virginia.edu/etcbin/toccer-new2?id=StoSojo.sgm&images=images/modeng&data=/texts/english/modeng/parsed&tag=public&part=1&division=div1.

3. W.T. Whalin, *Sojourner Truth: American Abolitionist* (Uhrichsville, OH: Barbour Publishing, Inc., 1997), 55–56.

Day 7 *The Moses of Her People: Harriet Tubman*

1. Judy Carlson, *Harriet Tubman: Call to Freedom* (New York, NY: Fawcett Columbine, 1989), 4.

2. Russell Smith, "Harriet Tubman: Moses of the Civil War."

3. Sarah Bradford, Harriet Tubman: *The Moses of Her People* (New York, NY: Corinth, 1969), 49–51.

DAY 8 *Overcoming Challenges: Aimee Semple McPherson*

1. Lately Thomas, *Storming Heaven* (New York, NY: William Morrow and Co., 1970), 20.

2. Edith L. Blumhofer, *Aimee Semple McPherson: Everybody's Sister* (New York, NY: William B. Eerdmans Publishing Company, 1993), 159–60.

3. Ibid., 161.

4. Geoff Thurling, *Aimee Semple McPherson* (Brisbane, Australia: Anointed for Revival, 1995), 3.

5. Daniel M. Epstein, *Sister Aimee* (New York, NY: Harcourt Brace Jovanovich, 1993), 206–207.

DAY 9 *The Peace of Jerusalem: Lydia Prince*

1. Ruth Prince, "Marriage and Ministry," *Derek Prince: His Life, His Work*, http://www.au.derekprince.com/mm.html.

2. Ibid.

3. Lydia and Derek Prince, *Appointment in Jerusalem* (Grand Rapids, MI: Chosen Books, 1975), 174. Used by permission. Derek Prince Ministries International, P.O. Box 19501, Charlotte, NC 28219-5901.

DAY 10 *Prelude to Revival: Bertha Smith*

1. Lewis Drummond, *Miss Bertha: Woman of Revival* (Nashville, TN: Broadman and Holman Publishers, 1996), 46.

2. Bertha Smith, *How the Spirit Filled My Life* (Nashville, TN: Broadman and Holman Publishers, 1973), 29.

3. Drummond, 40.

4. Ibid., 48–49.

5. C.L. Culpepper, *The Shantung Revival* (Dallas, TX: Crescendo Publications, 1971), 13–14.

6. Bertha Smith, *Go Home and Tell* (Nashville, TN: Broadman and Holman Publishers, 1995), 40.

DAY 11 *Saving God's People: Corrie ten Boom*

1. Corrie ten Boom, "The Hiding Place," in *Corrie ten Boom: Her Story* (New York, NY: Inspirational Press, a division of BBS Publishing Corporation, by arrangement with Chosen Books, Inc., and Fleming H. Revell, a division of Baker Book House Company, 1995).

DAY 12   *Turning Darkness into Light: Jackie Pullinger*

1. Jackie Pullinger, *Chasing the Dragon* (Ann Arbor, MI: Servant Books, 1982), 137.
2. Pullinger, *Crack in the Wall*, 8.
3. Pullinger, Chasing the Dragon, 34–36.

DAY 18   *Intimacy with God*

1. Francis Thompson, "The Hound of Heaven," Bartleby.com, http://www.bartleby.com/236/239.html.
2. John of the Cross, "The Living Flame of Love," www.karmel.at, http://www.karmel.at/ics/john/fl_3.html.

DAY 19   *Spiritual Intimacy: Madame Jeanne Guyon*

1. Jeanne Guyon, *Autobiography of Madame Guyon* (Pittsburgh, PA: Whitaker House, 1997), 7.
2. Ibid., 71-72.
3. Ibid., 61-64.
4. Ibid., 74.
5. Ibid.

DAY 20   *The Secret Place of Teresa of Avila*

1. Bob Lord and Penny Lord, *Saints and Other Powerful Women of the Church* (Westlake Village, CA: Journeys of Faith, 1989), 162.
2. Ibid.,178.
3. Tessa Bielecki, *Teresa of Avila: An Introduction to Her Life and Writings* (Kent, England: Burns & Oates, 1994), 20.
4. Lord, *Saints,* 178.
5. Lord, *Saints.*

DAY 21   *Powerful Songs: Fanny Crosby*

1. Bonnie C. Harvey, *Fanny Crosby* (Minneapolis, MN: Bethany House, 1999), 26.
2. Ibid., 55.

DAY 22   *Innovator and Educator: Susanna Wesley*

1. Kathy McReynolds, *Susanna Wesley* (Minneapolis, MN: Bethany House, 1998), 68–70.
2. Ibid., 94.

3. Ibid., 94.
4. Ibid., 95.
5. Bruce L. Shelley, *Church History in Plain Language* (Waco, TX: Word Books, 1982), 157–58.

Day 23   *The Sisterhood of Mary: Basilea Schlink*

1. Basilea Schlink, *I Found the Key to the Heart of God: My Personal Story* (Minneapolis, MN: Bethany House Publishers, 1975), 19.
2. Ibid., 33.
3. Ibid., 108.

Day 24   *End-Time Handmaidens: Gwen Shaw*

1. Gwen R. Shaw, *Share My Burden* (Jasper, AR: Engetal Press, 1984), 3.
2. Ibid., 2.
3. Ibid., 5.
4. Gwen R. Shaw, *Unconditional Surrender: My Life Story* (Jasper, AR: Engetal Press, 1986), 126.

Day 29   *Justice, Righteousness, and Compassion*

1. Charles H. Spurgeon, "The Compassion of Jesus" (sermon, Metropolitan Tabernacle, Newington, England, December 24, 1914).

Day 30   *The Power of Tears*

1. Dick Eastman, *No Easy Road* (Grand Rapids, MI: Baker Books, 1971), 93.
2. Ibid.

Day 32   *Beloved Woman of the Cherokee: Nancy Ward*

1. Written by Ada Winn with Dr. J. Mark Rodgers.
2. Pat Alderman, *Nancy Ward: Cherokee Chieftainess* (Johnson City, TN: Overmountain P, 1990). Very little is written about Nancy Ward except in this one source. The author of this chapter, Ada Winn, is a relative of Nancy Ward.
3. G. J. Barker-Benfield and Cathryn Clinton, eds., *Portraits of American Women from Settlement to the Present* (New York: Oxford University Press, 1998), 97.
4. *Ghighau* is a title for a certain woman in a tribe; it means "beloved woman."

Day 33   *More Than a Nurse: Florence Nightingale*

1. Basil Miller, *Florence Nightingale: The Lady of the Lamp* (New York, NY: Bethany House, 1987), 72.

2. Sam Wellman, *Florence Nightingale: Lady with the Lamp* (Uhrichsville, OH: Barbour, 1999), 58.

3. Ibid., 202.

Day 34   *Approved by God: Gladys Aylward*

1. Gladys Aylward and Christine Hunter, *Gladys Aylward: The Little Woman* (New York, NY: Moody, 1980), 42.

Day 35   *Paragon of Compassion: Mother Teresa*

1. Eileen Egan and Kathleen Egan, *Suffering into Joy: What Mother Teresa Teaches about True Joy* (Ann Arbor, MI: Servant Publications, 1994), 13.

2. Tore Frängsmyr, Mother Teresa, www.nobelprize.org, http://nobelprize.org /nobel_prizes/peace/laureates/1979/teresa-bio.html.

3. "Mother Teresa," www.wikipedia.org, http://en.wikipedia.org/wiki/Mother _Teresa#Missionaries_of_Charity.

4. Pope John Paul II (address, "The Beatification of Mother Teresa," The Vatican, Rome, Italy, 2003).

5. Egan, *Suffering into Joy*, 14.

6. Ibid., 22.

Day 36   *Five Empowered Women*

1. "Amy Carmichael," Dayspring Discipleship Institute, http:// dayspringdiscipleship.org/bioportraits/amycarmichael.html.

2. B. Trehane, *Fragments That Remain* (Fort Washington: CLC Publications, 2013), n.p.

3. American Saints, "St. Katherine Drexel," All for Mary, http://www. allformary.org/AmericanSaints/drexel.htm.

4. "Katharine Drexel," Vatican: The Holy See, http://www.vatican.va/news _services/liturgy/saints/ns_lit_doc_20001001_katharine-drexel_it.html.

5. "Elizabeth Fry," Spartacus Educational, http://www.spartacus.schoolnet .co.uk/REfry.htm.

Day 37   *Empowered Living: Heidi Baker*

1. Written by Julia C. Loren.

2. Rolland Baker and Heidi Baker, *There Is Always Enough* (Grand Rapids, MI: Sovereign Publishing, 2003), 26.

3. Ibid., 160.

4. Ibid., 164.
5. Ibid., 176–77.

Day 38 *Make It Personal*

1. Written by James W. Goll.
2. Mahesh Chavda, *Only Love Can Make a Miracle* (Ann Arbor, MI: Vine Books, 2002), 72–73.

Day 39 *Empowerment through Compassion*

1. Wesley Campbell, *Be a Hero: The Battle for Mercy and Social Justice* (Shippensburg, PA: Destiny Image, 2004), 165–68.
2. "Burma: World's Highest Number of Child Soldiers," Human Rights Watch, http://www.hrw.org/en/news/2002/10/15/burma-worlds-highest -number-child-soldiers.

About the Authors

MICHAL ANN GOLL was a lover of Jesus all her life, the devoted wife of James Goll for thirty-two years and mother of four beloved children. She was the founder of Compassion Acts, a member of the Debra Company Founder's Group, and honored to be listed in the Cambridge Who's Who. She traveled the globe demonstrating that love takes action. She authored eight books and co-established the Women on the Frontlines conferences. She graduated to her heavenly reward in the fall of 2008 and is greatly missed to this day by thousands of people around the world.

DR. JAMES W. GOLL is the president of God Encounters Ministries and is an international bestselling author, a certified Life Language Trainer, and has taught in more than fifty nations. James was married to Michal Ann for thirty-two years before her graduation to heaven in the fall of 2008. James has four adult children who are married and a growing number of grandchildren. James makes his home in Franklin, Tennessee.

Read More about These

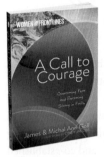

*W*omen throughout history have changed the world by their sacrifices, passion, and fire. *A Call to Courage* tells the inspiring stories of nine such women:

Joan of Arc, teenage peasant who led France's army against England, Vibia Perpetua, a martyr for her faith in the early church, Sojourner Truth, a leader in the anti-slavery movement, Harriet Tubman, a dedicated pioneer of the Underground Railroad during the Civil War, Aimee Semple McPherson, healing evangelist at the turn of the twentieth century, Lydia Prince, forerunner in caring for orphans and the purposes of God among the Jewish people, Bertha Smith, Baptist missionary and revival leader in China, Corrie ten Boom, Holocaust survivor who suffered for the cause of Christ and the Jewish people, and Jackie Pullinger, British evangelist and missionary in Hong Kong.

Heed the call to courage and step up to the front lines of faith, hope, and love!

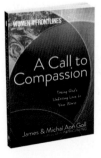

*J*esus lived and breathed compassion. He was and is compassion itself. *A Call to Compassion* is your personal invitation to discover the joy of committing your life to a cause higher than your own personal desires and learn to be a reflection of God's steadfast love. Be inspired by the stories of these eleven great women:

Great Women of Faith

Mother Teresa, devoted servant to the poor, Catherine Booth, cofounder of the Salvation Army, Nancy Ward, hero and "last beloved lady" of the Cherokee Nation, Florence Nightingale, reformer and pioneer of health care, Gladys Aylward, missionary to the sick, orphans, and poor in China, Amy Carmichael, missionary in India, Catherine Drexel, nun who gave away millions of dollars to help Native Americans and African Americans, Phoebe Palmer, mother of the Holiness Movement, Hannah More, well-known writer who worked for the abolition of slavery, Elizabeth Fry, prison reformer in England and Europe, and Heidi Baker, passionate missionary in Mozambique, Africa, and the world.

Be a pioneer of compassion in your world today!

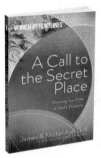

*D*eep inside each of us is a longing to escape the frantic pace of life. *A Call to the Secret Place* is your personal invitation to take that step toward the peace found in God's presence. Be inspired by:

Madam Guyon, influencial French writer on true union and intimacy with God, Teresa of Avila, Spanish Christian mystic who demonstrated intimate friendship with God, Susanna Wesley, innovator, educator, and mother of revival, Fanny Crosby, inspired songwriter of over nine thousand hymns, Basilea Schlink, German spiritual leader, writer, and founder of the Evangelical Sisterhood of Mary, Gwen Shaw, passionate minister carrying God's presence to the nations, and Elizabeth Alves, joyful intercessor and grandma of the prayer shield.

Come on in to fullfill your call to the secret place!

For More Information

James W. Goll
God Encounters Ministries
P.O. Box 1653
Franklin, TN 37065
Phone: 1–877–200–1604

Websites

GodEncounters.com • JamesGoll.com
CompassionActs.com • FreedomsPromise.org
woflglobal.com • PrayerStorm.com

E-mail

info@godencounters.com
cs@godencounters.com
classes@godencounters.com

Social Media

Facebook, Instagram, Twitter, GEM Media,
XPMedia, Kingdom Flame, YouTube, Vimeo,
Charisma Blog, and iTunes